The
Lhasa Apso

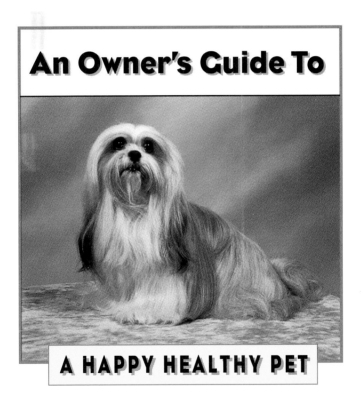

An Owner's Guide To

A HAPPY HEALTHY PET

Howell Book House

Howell Book House

A Simon & Schuster Macmillan Company

1633 Broadway

New York, NY 10019

Macmillan Publishing books may be purchased for business or sales promotional use. For information please write: Special Markets Department, Macmillan Publishing USA, 1633 Broadway, New York, NY 10019.

Library of Congress Cataloging-in-Publication Data

Herbel, Carolyn.

The lhasa apso-Carolyn Herbel.

   p.   cm. –(An owners's guide to a happy healthy pet)

Includes bibliographical references

ISBN: 0-87605-228-6

1. Lhasa apso. I. Title. II. Series.

SF429.L5H46   1998   98-17604

636.72—dc21   CIP

Manufactured in the United States of America

10 9 8 7 6 5 4 3 2 1

Series Director: Amanda Pisani

Series Assistant Director: Jennifer Liberts

Book Design: Michele Laseau

Cover Design: Iris Jeromnimon

Illustration: Patricia Douglas

Photography:

   Front cover photo and inset photo by Paulette Braun; back cover photo by Faith Uridel

   Paulette Braun: Title page, 2–3, 43, 70

   JoAnn Clulow: 9, 11, 52, 53

   Brona David: 27

   Carolyn Herbel: 5, 17, 18, 20, 21, 39, 41, 47

   Howell Book House (archival photos): 16

   Bob Schwartz: 13, 15, 19, 24, 25, 33, 40, 51, 68

   Sara Sechrest: 75, 93

   Toni Tucker: 45, 69

   Faith Uridel: 7, 8, 23, 30–31, 32, 37, 44, 56, 57, 58, 59, 60, 61, 64

Production Team: David Faust, Clint Lahnen, Dennis Sheehan, Terri Sheehan, Chris Van Camp

Contents

Welcome
to the
World

of the
Lhasa
Apso

External Features of the Lhasa Apso

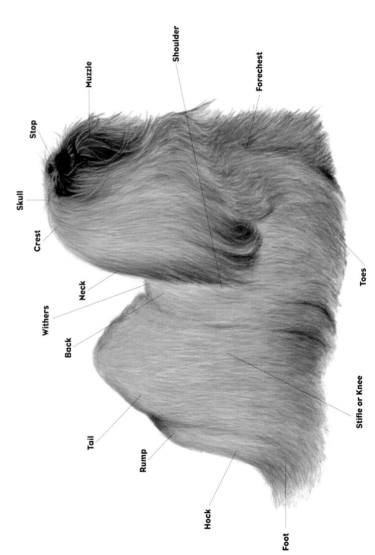

Skull

Crest

Stop

Muzzle

Shoulder

Forechest

Neck

Withers

Back

Tail

Rump

Hock

Foot

Stifle or Knee

Toes

chapter 1

What Is a Lhasa Apso ?

The Lhasa Apso is a small, spirited canine with long hair covering him from head to tail. The Lhasa Apso originates from the remote country of Tibet where he was a companion and a small indoor guard dog. Tibet was a relatively primitive country, and survival was the primary concern of both the people and the animals that inhabited it. Out of this environment came the Lhasa Apso, who developed into a naturally hardy watchdog with an especially discerning temperament.

The Breed Standard

The American Lhasa Apso standard describes the behavior and appearance of the Lhasa Apso and was first approved by the American Kennel Club in 1935. A substantial part of the American standard was derived from the original English standard (which was adopted in 1934 when the English Tibetan Breeds Association defined and divided the Tibetan breeds). At about this time the English Kennel Club also declared that Lhasa Terriers (later renamed Lhasa Apsos) and Shih Tzus were not the same breed, and therefore would be registered separately.

The American Lhasa Apso standard remained unchanged for forty-three years and was only slightly revised in 1978 when the gold coat color preference was removed, making all coat colors equally acceptable; the preference for the slightly undershot bite was made equal to the preference for the level mouth; and the preference for a 1-inch muzzle length was removed.

The American standard is divided into a list of twelve categories, which is very brief when compared to the other breed standards. Some people speculate that the standard is actually a list of traits that describe the little dog from Tibet and also those traits that differentiate the Lhasa Apso from the Shih Tzu.

CHARACTER

Gay and assertive, but chary of strangers.

The authors of the standard must have felt that the character of the Lhasa Apso was distinctly important because the first statement describes the Lhasa Apso as a dog that has a happy, confident temperament and chooses new friends carefully. The word assertive can equate to stubbornness in some Lhasa Apsos, while in most it simply means an assured character. As a result of the Lhasa Apsos' longtime indoor sentry work in Tibet, they are extraordinarily alert and quick to give warning of anything unusual. The Lhasa Apso may be standoffish with strangers; however, many have developed a more friendly attitude because they share common ancestors with the amiable Shih Tzu. The Lhasa Apso is very sensitive to the moods of his owner and responds accordingly. He likes to be with his human family, but does not act as an obedient servant because he considers himself an equal member of the family. A typical Lhasa Apso does not live for you—he lives with you.

A good way to evaluate the possible future temperament of a Lhasa Apso puppy is to interact with his parents. The parents should not be high-strung or aggressive. Most Lhasa Apso puppies are friendly to strangers until they are about 6 months old, when they usually become more discerning about making friends. If puppies act fearful or aggressive at a much younger age, it may mean that they will be even more reluctant to accept strangers when they mature.

The Lhasa Apso is a happy, confident dog who is sensitive to his owner's moods.

Lhasas and Children

Lhasa Apsos that are raised from puppyhood with well-behaved children love them. Not all Lhasa Apsos, however, readily accept the quick movements, hair pulling and unsure footsteps of toddlers, unless they have been introduced to these little people first.

SIZE

Variable, but about ten inches or eleven inches at shoulder for dogs; bitches slightly smaller.

The size standard is only defined by height. The word *variable* means that the height of the Lhasa Apso varies between 10 and 11 inches, and the word *about* means that there is an allowance above and below the 10 or 11 inches designated in the standard. *Bitches slightly smaller* means that females should not only be smaller, but should also have feminine traits. Another category in the standard that pertains to size is the proportion and condition of body shape.

BODY SHAPE

The length from point of shoulders to point of buttocks longer than height at withers, well ribbed up, strong loin, well developed quarters and thighs.

The description of height, proportion and body shape in the standard was most likely determined by observing the structure of Lhasa Apsos in Tibet as well as those that were imported to England and the United States. The description of length means that when viewed from the side, the Lhasa Apso should look distinctly rectangular, not square shaped. Though weight is not mentioned in the standard, well-conditioned Lhasa Apsos with strong loins, quarters and thighs should weigh 16 to 18 pounds for males and 12 to 14 pounds for females.

The shape of the Lhasa Apso should be rectangular rather than square.

Certainly larger and smaller dogs existed in Tibet, yet appraisal of the small Tibetan watchdog known as the Lhasa Apso determined the size description in the standard. Deviating more than ½ inch from this desired height starts to change the efficient, hardy body structure and handy indoor size developed due to the Tibetan environment. The choice of a pet should not be made entirely on size, but it is important to see the parents in order to approximate the size your puppy may be as an adult. If one of the deciding factors for choosing a Lhasa Apso is that they are small dogs, it would be disappointing to have your puppy grow much larger than you expected.

COLORS

All colors equally acceptable with or without dark tips to ears and beard.

The original English and American standards listed colors in order of preference: "(T)his being the true Tibetan Lion-dog, golden or lionlike colors are preferred." The preference for golden or lionlike colors developed because this was the color that the Western travelers saw and liked the most during visits to Tibet—especially in the capital city of Lhasa from which most of the dogs came from. Parti-color was probably among the least preferred colors because this color pattern was more often associated with the Shih Tzu. In 1978, the color section of the standard was changed to make all colors of equal value.

Black and tan is one of the AKC's standard Lhasa Apso colors.

The standard colors that appear on the AKC's individual registration form are black; black and tan; cream; golden; grizzle; red; red gold and white. The second choice in describing a color is the marking/pattern portion of the form, which consists of black mask with tips; black tips; brindle; parti-color; sable and white markings.

The definitions of the standard colors and markings/patterns are as follows:

- **Black**—solid black

- **Black and tan**—typical black and tan markings, i.e., black body color with tan spots above eyes, on eyes, cheeks, muzzle, chest, legs and vent

- **Cream**—almost white to darker shades of cream

- **Golden**—pale gold to wheaten

- **Grizzle**—bluish-gray or iron-gray color due to a mixture of black and white hairs

- **Red**—solid red with shades from Viszla red to Irish Setter red to light red

- **Red gold**—dark apricot to light red

- **White**—solid white

- **Black mask with tips**—dark shading of varying degrees about the head, ears, legs, and tails, i.e., dark points

- **Black tips**—black-tipped hairs, i.e., sable

- **Brindle**—a color pattern produced by the presence of darker hairs forming bands and giving a striped effect on a background of cream, gold or red

- **Parti-color**—a color pattern broken up into two or more colors, one of which is white, in more or less equal proportions

- **Sable**—a color pattern produced by black-tipped hairs overlaid upon a background of gold, cream, red or red gold

- **White markings**—white on colored background usually on one or a combination of legs, cheek, collar, blaze, muzzle or tail tip

Additionally, the AKC provides alternate color descriptions to be written on the line at the bottom of the color section. These alternate definitions are as follows:

- **Gray**—light charcoal or blue or grizzle

- **Silver**—a mixture of cream and black, charcoal or gray, i.e., cream sable or cream grizzle

- **Liver** (or brown or chocolate)—deep reddish brown with liver-colored pigment
- **Charcoal**—dark slate gray, i.e., faded black
- **Blue**—a dilution of black, either light or dark blue gray with self-colored blue skin pigment
- **Sable with white markings**—this is a combination of two marking/pattern descriptions and needs only to have a standard color added to identify the sable base color

Although there are many colors from which to pick, a Lhasa Apso should never be chosen only for his color because proper temperament and sound health is much more important when selecting a family pet.

COAT

Heavy, straight, hard, not woolly or silky, of good length and very dense.

The Lhasa Apso's coat is described by its texture and value in the standard. A correct coat is probably one of the Lhasa Apso's most important survival features. A *heavy* coat means that the coat has weight and when it

Lhasa Apsos usually have long whiskers and a beard.

is lifted away from the body, it falls quickly back into place. The coat should never be a soft, fine, light or flyaway texture. A *hard* coat means the coat should be strong, resilient and durable. The hair should not break off easily or be silky, thin or fragile. *Straight* suggests not curly, kinky or woolly. *Of good length* means that the coat should be long enough to protect the Lhasa Apso from extreme weather. *Very dense* means that there should be a good quality of the heavy, straight, hard outer coat

and enough soft undercoat to keep the body protected from extreme temperatures.

The standard suggests that the coat around the head should be heavy . . . with good fall over eyes, good whiskers and beard. The coat around the ears should be heavily feathered; the legs: both forelegs and hind legs heavily furnished with hair; the feet and tail sections: well-feathered—all simply describing the fact that the Lhasa Apso is covered with coat from head to tail and from ears to feet.

Usually the puppy with a hard, heavy, shorter coat will have the best-quality adult coat. Although the puppy with a soft, fluffy coat is often the most appealing, he will require daily grooming or routine shearing as an adult (especially if he runs in the yard or participates with the family in activities like walking in the park, going fishing or hiking in the woods).

HEAD

Skull narrow, falling away behind the eyes in a marked degree, not quite flat, but not domed or apple-shaped; straight foreface of fair length. Nose black, the length from tip of nose to eye to be roughly about one-third of the total length from nose to back of skull.

Other sections that should be included when discussing the head are:

Eyes
Dark brown, neither very large and full, nor very small and sunk.

Ears
Pendant, heavily feathered.

Mouth and Muzzle
The preferred bite is either level or slightly undershot. Muzzle of medium length; a square muzzle is objectionable.

The Lhasa Apso should not have large, bulging eyes that can be damaged easily, or an obstructed airway that would make breathing difficult. The ears, covered with protective hair, should be rather small and carried somewhat close to the head. The type of bite is not of concern as long as it is healthy and not overshot excessively or undershot. Although it is not suitable for show, faulty occlusions usually will not negatively affect the pet. This portion of the standard definitely distinguishes the Lhasa Apso's head from the domed skull, short, square muzzle and broad round head of the Shih Tzu.

LEGS AND FEET

In addition to being covered with hair, forelegs are defined by the standard as *straight* and feet as *round and catlike with good pads*. These are traits that assisted the Lhasa Apso to survive in Tibet and still enables him to be an active, healthy and sturdy pet.

TAIL AND CARRIAGE

In addition to being well-feathered, the tail *should be carried well over back in a screw; there may be a kink at the end. A low carriage of stern is a serious fault.* This portion of the standard is easily understood when the uncommon usage of several words is explained. The term *screw* means the curls in the tail; *kink* means a bend in the tail bones and *stern* is another word for tail.

The issue of proper tail carriage has been in question for many years (with a low carriage enough to be considered a serious fault). The various theories regarding this quandary are fascinating. For example, an article authored by Tibetan breeds expert Mr. Lionel Jacobs and published in the December 1901 *Kennel Gazette* stated that the "stern . . . should be carried well over the back after the manner of the tail of the Chow. All Tibetan dogs carry their tail in this way, and a low carriage of stern is a sign of impure blood." Other

A Lhasa Apso will carry his tail well over his back if he is happy and energetic, and will let his tail drop when he is relaxed.

13

theories suggest that the tail carried over the back was akin to an umbrella and shaded the little dog from the sun in the high altitude of Tibet; or the tail shaded and protected the dog's body while he was sleeping, and should therefore be carried high and away from harm.

The tail carriage is affected most by the Lhasa Apso's state of mind. Perhaps the authors of the standard inadvertently emphasized the correct character of the Lhasa Apso by ending the standard with the description of tail carriage, because a Lhasa Apso that is gay and assertive will usually carry his tail well over the back. If a Lhasa Apso is relaxed, startled or ill at ease, the tail probably will be dropped yet should come up well over the back when the Lhasa Apso is alert or has regained his composure.

The Lhasa Apso that is bred by a breeder, who uses the standard as a blueprint for his or her breeding program, should be a hardy, sturdy and long-lived pet with few health problems.

chapter 2

The Lhasa Apso's Ancestry

The Lhasa Apso evolved due to her ability to survive in the uncompromising and remote environment of Tibet, where the average altitude is 16,000 feet, with climatic extremes ranging from extremely arid and dry to terribly cold and wet. Because there is virtually no historical record and Tibetan society was inaccessible to Westerners for many years, we have very little fact and much conjecture about the Tibetan Lhasa Apso's origin. It is believed that Lhasas developed, for the most part, from the primal dog—there is no documentation of planned breeding  of ancestral breeds for the purpose of creating the small Tibetan breed we now know as the Lhasa Apso.

An Ancient Breed

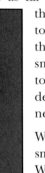

Welcome to the World of the Lhasa Apso

The Lhasa Apso is probably related to the ancient Asiatic guarding and herding dogs that were completely covered with hair from head to tail and used by primitive man as far back as 800 B.C. Although their nomadic herding ancestors were conceivably larger, the Lhasa Apso's size became smaller as Tibetans started to settle in permanent residences. Lhasas then filled the need for indoor guard dogs.

With the introduction of the smaller Tibetan dogs to the Western world, names like Bhuteer Terrier, Bhutese Dog, Lhassa Terrier, Lhasa Tibetan Terrier, Thibetan or Tibetan Terrier, Apso, Tibetan or Lhasa Apso, Tibetan Spaniel, Tibetan or Chinese Lion Dog and Shih Tzu were linked with their history. Westerners tended to name newly discovered breeds after the area where the dog was believed to have originated, thus many of these names were used for the same breed. The dogs were further classified into familiar groups like spaniels or terriers.

Ch. Licos Kulu La.

FAMOUS OWNERS OF THE LHASA APSO

Richard Burton

Phyllis Diller

Eva Gabor

Peggy Guggenheim

Bob Hope

Liberace

Bob Mackie

Susan Strasberg

Elizabeth Taylor

Jonathan Taylor Thomas

THE LHASA APSO NAME

The name Lhasa Apso is taken from Lhasa, the capital city of Tibet, and according to early documents, from where the best specimens of the breed originated. The word Apso is undeniably Tibetan yet because of translation difficulty there is much speculation about the true meaning of the word Apso. It's possibly a corruption of Tibetan word *rapso,* which loosely translates to "goatlike" and depicts the similarity of the Lhasa Apso to small, long-coated Tibetan goats. Another comparable Tibetan word is *abso,* which roughly translates to "bark sentinel," while other suggestions are that the word simply means "covered all over with hair."

Many scholars of Tibetan canines believe that the Tibetan people did not distinguish between breeds as explicitly as Westerners did, nor did they plan breeding as intently. The breeds that we are familiar with today that look most like their ancestors are the Kyi Apso, the Tibetan Terrier and the Lhasa Apso. Size reduction in the Tibetan Spaniel resulted in slightly bowed front legs and a coat pattern similar to early pictures of the Pekingese. The Shih Tzu's broad skull and flat-faced appearance also suggests an influence from Chinese breeders, who bred for more aesthetic than intrinsic purposes.

The Tibetans commonly called their little dogs Seng Kyi or Seng Tru, names that were interpreted by Westerners to mean "lion dog" and "lion cub." Some other popular names for Tibetan dogs were Rgyal-Po (king), Rgyal-Mo (queen), Rgyal-Bu (prince), Me-Tog (flower), Cun-Ba or Nyun-Ba (little), Kan-Da (candy), On-Ba (charming), Tob-Ci (button), Bar-Ba (blossom), Yter (treasure), Ser-Po (yellow), Yser (gold), Dmar-Po (red) and Pad-Ma (lotus).

The Lhasa Apso arrived in America in the early 1930s.

The Lhasa's Arrival in England and America

The Lhasa Apso emigrated to England in the 1890s, but it was not until the early 1930s that Mr. and Mrs. C. Suydam Cutting of Hamilton Farms in New Jersey

Welcome to the
World of the
Lhasa Apso

brought Lhasa Apsos directly from Tibet to the United States. Mr. Cutting, a world traveler, visited Tibet and received gifts including Lhasa Apsos from both the thirteenth and fourteenth Dalai Lamas. It was also during this time that Shi Tzus were imported to the United States from Canada and England and registered by the American Kennel Club as Lhasa Apsos, a practice that continued until the late 1950s.

APPROVAL OF THE AMERICAN LHASA APSO STANDARD

The American Lhasa Apso standard was first approved by the AKC in 1935, and was essentially copied from the original English standard. The English standard was developed from excerpts of two English documents from the *Kennel Gazette* magazine: a description of the "Bhuteer Terrier" published in 1901 and the judge's critique of "Apsos," March 1934. Mr. G. Hayes, breeds judge for the 1934 Crufts' Dog Show, wrote the critique.

The American Lhasa Apso Club became active in Obedience Trials in the 1980s.

THE AMERICAN LHASA APSO CLUB

The American Lhasa Apso Club (ALAC) was founded on February 9, 1959, during the Westminster Kennel Club show in New York City. Fourteen members answered the first roll call, and sixty-one fanciers had registered to be members. C. Suydam Cutting, Hamilton Farms, was the honorary president, a position he held until his death in 1972. Mr. Cutting's kennel manager, the late Fred Huyler, was the first president and treasurer.

The first ALAC sanctioned match was held in September 1962 on the grounds of Hamilton Farms. Thirty-eight Lhasa Apsos participated in this historic event. The first ALAC specialty show, with an entry of fifty-two, was held in May 1966. In 1969, ALAC received permission from the AKC to have two specialty shows a year. Known as the Eastern and Western Specialties, they were sponsored by ALAC until 1980, when the membership approved one roving National Specialty to be held in various regions of the country.

Today the Lhasa Apso is a popular show dog.

In 1983, ALAC was licensed to host an Obedience Trial, and for the first time obedience classes were held in conjunction with conformation classes at the annual Specialty Show. ALAC continues to sponsor the annual Specialty Show and Obedience Trial, which is held the third week in June each year with an average entry of 200 dogs. Other activities added to this yearly convention are the awards dinner, sweepstakes, futurity, canine good citizen testing and annual meetings.

ALAC also sponsors Health and Educational committees, a Measurement Certification Program and publishes a yearbook and a newsletter.

chapter 3

The **World** According to the Lhasa Apso

The Lhasa Apso's comparatively small size makes him suitable for city residents with limited yard space. His tendency to lounge quietly where he can see his favorite family member makes the Lhasa Apso a great pet for a small apartment or a multifamily building.

All About Lhasas

Lhasa Apsos can be quite content being indoors for most of their lives and seem to retain good muscular condition just by running around the house. When a Lhasa Apso has the attention of his family, he may race around like an exhibitionist just for the family's amusement, revealing his sense of humor. Lhasas are also sensitive to the family members' feelings and know when to be quiet.

They know instinctively when the family is not in the mood for games. Most do not seem to need an inordinate amount of exercise but can enjoy a brisk walk or a romp in the park with the people they love if this is a part of their regular routine. If not introduced to activities outside the home when young, Lhasa Apsos tend to be uncomfortable away from home.

Long-Lived

The Lhasa Apso is generally a healthy breed that lives an average of sixteen years. Because the breed is noted for living a long time, he is somewhat slower to mature than many other breeds; therefore, Lhasa Apso puppies should not go to new homes until they are at least 12 weeks old. Generally an adult Lhasa Apso makes an excellent pet and usually requires much less training than a young puppy. Elderly Apsos (over 9 years of age) can, however, have some difficulty adjusting well to a different home

with new people, new places and new routines. This is heightened by the breed's homebody temperament, so please remember this and consider your new puppy's lifelong needs when selecting the Lhasa Apso.

Lhasa Apsos are happy to play independently with a favorite toy.

Independent and Playful

The typical Lhasa Apso's personality resembles that of a cat in many ways. He has an independent attitude and commonly plays by batting his toy and pouncing on it or chasing it across the floor and biting to "kill" the prey. Most Lhasa Apsos like playing and jumping on and off of high places. Allowing Lhasa Apsos to play on high open decks can be dangerous because they seem to have no fear of heights.

The Temperamental Lhasa

Welcome to the
World of the
Lhasa Apso

A Lhasa Apso with typical temperament lives *with* his family, not *for* his family, and this attitude can sometimes equate to stubbornness or even aggressiveness in an attempt to be the alpha member of his family. Regardless of age, any growling or snapping at a family member attempting to take a toy, chew bone or food from a Lhasa Apso should be met with definite disapproval. The independent nature or stubbornness of some Lhasa Apsos can be reflected in housebreaking difficulty although more often than not it is a lack of proper training that creates disobedience.

> **CHARACTERISTICS OF A LHASA APSO**
>
> Loving
>
> Playful
>
> Poor swimmer
>
> Independent
>
> Long, thick, straight hair
>
> Barks when warning or guarding

Unfortunately Lhasa Apsos have a reputation for biting and aggressiveness among some veterinarians, animal care specialists and professional groomers. Lhasa Apsos that display this inappropriate behavior are probably the result of inconsistent discipline and incorrect behavioral training. An aggressive or biting Lhasa Apso should not be tolerated, especially when there are children involved. There are reasons an Apso bites, but few excuses. An Apso that bites the hands that feed him is contrary to the nature of the species.

LHASA APSOS AND CHILDREN

Small children should be taught to respect the rights of the Lhasa Apso. When children are taught to be gentle and loving the Lhasa Apso will reciprocate. While Apsos are a hardy breed, they should not be regarded as a stuffed toy or a wrestling partner for young children.

CONFRONTATIONS WITH OTHER ANIMALS

Although comparatively small, the Lhasa Apso is independent and will not usually back down from a fight, so protect him from any risk of injury by preventing confrontations with other animals. The typical Lhasa Apso sees himself as a large animal.

Obedience classes are an excellent way for a family to learn how to communicate properly with their Lhasa Apso. In special cases, sessions with a pet behavioral counselor may be necessary. Be sure the counselor you select understands the character of Lhasa Apsos because some behavior modification techniques, like pronged collars, probably will not be successful with this breed. Lhasa Apsos are usually receptive to discipline if it is done justly. Apsos, like children, require instruction in order to understand what is appropriate behavior. Remember that if a particular behavior is not acceptable for an adult dog, do not allow it to go undisciplined in a puppy.

Lhasas need training at an early age, and training should be reinforced as they mature.

Finding a Good Match

A situation that sometimes leads to aggressiveness in Apsos is the mismatching of human and canine personalities. Lhasa Apsos with strong, willful personalities belong with families who are willing and capable of enforcing appropriate discipline. These Apsos usually do well in active homes, with or without children, where constant change keeps them occupied and suitably stimulated. Place a strong-willed Apso with a senior couple who want only to baby him and this unguided Apso will attempt to run the home and will actually boss his owners by demanding and denying attention at will. This Apso often becomes destructive when left to his own devises as if to punish his humans for leaving him without their attention. With the mentality of

Welcome to the
World of the
Lhasa Apso

a 3-year-old child, the dog isn't wise, and his dog-logic contains the only tools available—growl, bite and bark—all tools of aggression, which inflict discomfort to humans.

Conversely, the quiet, even shy, Apso does well in a tranquil home, usually with seniors or families with older children. These Apsos respond to gentle discipline, love to be babied and are content when left alone. However, place this quiet puppy in a home with four children under 10 years old and he turns into a wall-hugging fear biter, cringing when grabbed and wary of participating in loud activities.

A Sentinel Breed

As you have read several times in this book, the Lhasa Apso is a sentinel breed, and as such uses his bark to do his job. Though not a "yappy" dog by nature, Apsos make sure their families hear their bark whenever something out of the ordinary occurs. A stranger at the door, a new noise in the house, a newly delivered carton in the middle of the room, a fallen object or person and even a fire will trigger the sentinel Apso to sound alarm for his owner. The bark alarm is a trait that every Lhasa Apso owner should expect and appreciate because it is one of the very reasons that the Tibetan people loved and held their Apsos in high esteem. The bark should be an expected characteristic, much like swimming is to the Labrador Retriever or running is to the Greyhound.

Your Lhasa Apso will use his bark to alert you to anything out of the ordinary.

Living with a Lhasa Apso means that as a bark sentinel he will quietly observe and alert you only of those things that are strange by barking or growling. He should be friendly with people he knows, but cautious about strangers and unfamiliar conditions. The dog should not bark unchecked, indeed, the sentinel's job is done when the owner takes over the situation.

Some misguided owners will give a barking Lhasa Apso a treat, hoping to quiet him, an action that only reinforces this behavior because he is learning that if he barks he will be rewarded with a biscuit. Stroking and sweet-talking is considered encouragement to a growling Apso because although the owner is hoping to calm the dog, the Apso views theses kind words and stroking as validation of his behavior. Tolerating such behavior may turn a willful Lhasa into an aggressive dog.

When barking becomes a problem, several training methods can be incorporated into a training regimen for either adults or puppies. Lhasa Apso puppies are often overly zealous in sounding alarm and will need to be trained to know the difference between acceptable bark sentinel noise and undesirable noise. With persistent guidance, a Lhasa Apso puppy will usually have better judgment about when you need to be warned as he develops his mature personality. Many barking problems are not due to a "bad" Apso, but are instead due to lack of training. With training, excessive barking should be eliminated in due time.

Brush your Lhasa immediately after he exercises outdoors in order to remove debris that can cause tangles or irritation.

The Lhasa's Coat Care

The Lhasa Apso has long hair similar to thick, straight human hair. He also has a soft undercoat that varies in amount depending on the temperature. The Lhasa Apso does not shed perpetually as do shorter coated breeds, and if groomed regularly generally does not irritate people who are allergic to dogs. The Lhasa Apso sheds a bit all the time, though less when groomed regularly.

This loss of hair compares in amount to the natural loss of hair humans experience. Once or twice a year,

Welcome to the
World of the
Lhasa Apso

usually when seasonal changes are extreme, the under-coat will loosen and wrap around the outer coat. During this time there is more of a tendency for tangling, and more brushing is necessary.

Because the Lhasa Apso is a long-coated breed, there are choices to be made in regard to the coat length and care. In chapter 6, complete instructions for grooming have been provided; however, here are some suggestions that will make coat care easier. When your Lhasa Apso exercises in an area where the coat collects dried leaves, burrs, twigs, grass seeds or clippings, this debris should be removed immediately because it can create tangles or cause irritation to the skin. A rain-soaked Lhasa Apso should be brushed dry under a hair dryer to eliminate matting. His rear coat may become soiled with fecal matter and should be checked after each exercising (potty) time.

The Lhasa Apso generally likes cold weather better than hot weather and will frequently stand facing into a frigid north wind. Even though the Lhasa Apso seems to enjoy cold weather, if his coat is clipped short (less than 3 inches long), a sweater may be needed to replace the protection his natural coat would give him.

Traveling

Lhasa Apsos that have traveled with their owners since puppyhood like to ride. When taking your Lhasa Apso in the car always put him in a protective travel crate. Although it may be fun to have your Lhasa Apso loose on a seat near you, this is not safe because you may be distracted by his actions or slow to apply the brakes suddenly for fear of slamming him against the dashboard or onto the floor. Additionally, if there is a car accident, the dog may be injured by being thrown around in the car.

Observe the weather before you take your Lhasa Apso on a trip so that you do not submit him to extremes of temperature. If you have to leave your Lhasa alone in the car, it should be for a very short time. Always lock the car with the windows slightly open to allow ventilation. **Never leave your pet alone in a car when the weather is warm and the sun is shining.** When these conditions exist, the oxygen supply can quickly be depleted and the temperature can rise to well over 100°F. This can be sure death for your pet.

Male or Female?

Both female and male Lhasa Apsos make excellent family pets. It is strongly recommended that you have your dog neutered or spayed. Having your female spayed will eliminate the responsibility, three times a year, of keeping her confined for three weeks while she is in season. A male will not want to roam in search of a female nor will he tend to develop an overly dominant attitude if he is neutered. Generally, individual Lhasa Apsos get along well

With mutual respect, children and Lhasa Apsos can become great friends.

with each other and with other household animals; however, altering the pet will help to ensure compatibility, particularly with dogs of the same sex. The matter of mating the Lhasa Apso should be the responsibility of experienced, knowledgeable and properly equipped breeders.

Lhasas Like Routine

Occasionally, a Lhasa Apso that has been the sole pet in a household resents a newcomer with whom he must share the attention. A newcomer can be a new baby, a new spouse, a grandparent or another pet. Also, an "only child" Lhasa Apso can be upset by lifestyle changes such as death, divorce or a long-distance family move. This resentment or upset may be revealed by a lapse in housebreaking, unexpected aggression or moping. This upset is particularly aggravated if the Lhasa Apso's access to the household is curtailed.

Welcome to the
World of the
Lhasa Apso

Include the Lhasa Apso in household changes and he will usually accept the change more readily.

Snoring

Some Lhasa Apsos snore, but this is not a characteristic that is common if the head and muzzle are properly structured. Lhasa Apsos that snore usually have the tendency toward brachycephalic features: shorter muzzles, pinched nostrils and broader skulls.

Not Good Swimmers

Keep your Lhasa Apso away from bodies of water like swimming pools or fish ponds, unless the water is so shallow that he can walk out of it. If he is not rescued at the first sign of weakness, the Lhasa may drown. Even though individual Lhasa Apsos like water, the breed is not known for their swimming prowess and, with a long coat, can be weighed down and lose stamina quickly.

More Information on Lhasa Apsos

NATIONAL BREED CLUB

American Lhasa Apso Club, Inc.
Amy Andrews, Breeder Referral
18105 Kirkshire
Beverly Hills, MI 48025

Lynn Jamison, Education and Health
801 Linda Lane
Raymore, MO 64083-9207

Mary Schroeder, Breed Rescue
5395 S. Miller St.
Littleton, CO 80127

Joyce Johanson, Membership
126 Kurlene Dr.
Macomb, IL 61455

BOOKS

Herbel, Norman and Carolyn. *The New Complete Lhasa Apso.* New York: Howell Book House, 1992.

Vervaeke-Helf, Sally Ann. *Lhasa Lore.* Loveland, Colo.: Alpine Publications, 1983.

Wehrmann, Stephen. *Lhasa Apsos.* Hauppauge, N.Y.: Barron's Educational Series, Inc., 1990.

MAGAZINES

The Lhasa Bulletin
(Published bimonthly by the American
Lhasa Apso Club)
JoAnn Germano, Editor
85 DeForest Ave.
West Islip, NY 11795

The Lhasa Apso Reporter
Denise Olejniczak, Editor and Publisher
7465 Van Dyke
Romeo, MI 48065

VIDEOS

Lhasa Apsos. The American Kennel Club.

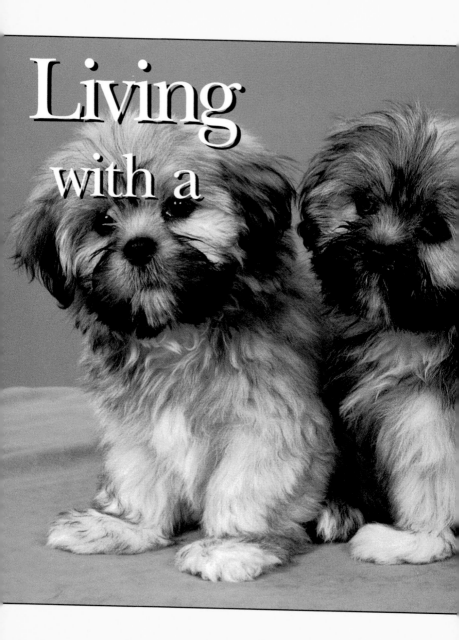

Living
with a

part two

Lhasa Apso

chapter 4

Bringing Your Lhasa Apso Home

Choosing a family dog requires extensive research. You should plan for this new family member to be in your household for many years. You are not only obligated to love and play with this new dog but are also required to commit a substantial amount of time and money to training and caring for your dog for her entire life. Careful planning before making your selection will help avoid having to live with a dog who is not suitable for your household.

Advance Planning

Before you go shopping, read the first part of this book. Next, look at your environment and try to envision it containing a Lhasa Apso. If after this deliberation you feel that a Lhasa Apso is the breed for you and your family, it is time to select your dog.

Once you've decided upon a Lhasa Apso, then you should consider if your lifestyle suits a puppy or an adult dog.

ADULT DOG OR PUPPY?

You will need to decide whether to get an adult, a puppy, a male or a female. Young puppies are appealing because they are cute, have few opinions, seem to like everything and are usually more responsive to you than more mature Lhasa Apsos. Adult Lhasa Apsos may take more time to adjust and get to know you at first.

With an adult, you have the opportunity to determine characteristics like personality, size, color and coat texture, while with puppies these traits are less certain. Most likely an adult is housetrained and will need only to have the reinforcement of patience and guidance once she is in her new home. Although a puppy should have started her housetraining with the breeder, she may be only paper-trained. Because of the stages of teething the puppy will go through, she will need diligent supervision so that she does not chew on something that is dangerous or valuable.

If an adult dog appeals to you, research her background and inquire as to why she is no longer in her previous home. If she lost her home because of bad habits, you need to know this before you adopt her.

Where to Find a Lhasa Apso

Shopping for your new Lhasa Apso should be fun; however, shopping can be risky. The risk is falling for the first cute face you see and forgetting to consider all the factors needed to make this experience successful for many years. Make a list of the important things to consider, take it with you when you shop for your new Lhasa Apso and refer to it before making a commitment. This list should help you to choose with your head as well as your heart.

BREEDERS

Local breed clubs, local specialty clubs or local dog shows may have lists of Lhasa Apso breeders from whom you can get information about the availability of Lhasa Apsos. Another source of adult Lhasa Apsos, especially females, is from show breeders who have limited space. After a female has had a litter or two, she may be released from the breeding program. These females make great pets because they have been living in a family situation while being shown and bred. Also, puppies and young adults of both sexes are frequently available from show breeders because they did not develop the characteristics expected for showing or breeding. These dogs are usually housetrained, socialized and make happy, well-adjusted pets. Ask for the dog's health record so that you can supply your veterinarian with this information.

VETERINARIANS

Veterinarians can be excellent sources for names of Lhasa Apso breeders in your area. Your choice of a veterinarian should be made before you bring your Lhasa Apso home; therefore, visiting local veterinarians can serve two purposes—finding local Lhasa Apso breeders and making an evaluation that will help you choose a veterinarian for your Lhasa Apso.

AKC Registration

If you buy a Lhasa Apso that is represented as being eligible for registration with the American Kennel Club

(AKC), you are entitled to receive an AKC application form properly filled out by the seller. This will enable you to register the dog by completing the application and submitting it to the AKC with the proper fee. When the application has been processed, you will receive an AKC registration certificate.

Under AKC rules, any person who sells dogs that are represented as being eligible for AKC registration must maintain records that will make it possible to give full identifying information with every dog delivered, even though AKC papers may not yet be available. *Do not accept a promise of later identification.*

The Rules and Regulations of The American Kennel Club stipulate that whenever someone sells or delivers a dog that is purported to be eligible for registration with the AKC, the dog must be identified either by presenting the buyer with a properly completed AKC registration application, or by giving the buyer a bill of sale or a written statement signed by the seller, giving the dog's full breeding information as follows:

- Breed, sex and color of the dog
- Date of birth of the dog
- Registered names of the dog's sire and dam
- Name of the breeder

If you encounter any problems getting the necessary registration application forms, write to the American Kennel Club, Attention: Registration, 5580 Centerview Dr., Raleigh, NC 27606-3390, giving as much information as possible regarding your situation, and the problem will be reviewed. All individuals acquiring a dog represented as being eligible for AKC registration should realize that it is their responsibility to obtain identification of the dog that is sufficient to satisfy AKC records. If these records are not available, *the dog should not be purchased.*

Many breeders utilize the limited registration, an option provided by the American Kennel Club. The limitation means that although the Lhasa Apso is registered, he or she cannot be used for breeding. It should make no difference to you if your Lhasa Apso's breeder has chosen to limit her registration because you are adopting a pet and should be planning to alter her.

PEDIGREE
The pedigree is not an official document of registration but is a record of your Lhasa Apso's ancestors, and you should be supplied with this document along with the official AKC registration form.

Rescue Organizations
Another source of adult dogs, and occasionally puppies, is from rescue organizations. These organizations are the connection between dogs that have lost their homes and people who want a new pet. You may be able to adopt an adult Lhasa Apso because a crisis in her family has made it impossible for her to stay in her present home.

Create a Support System
Before you bring your Lhasa Apso home, you need to have an established support group that consists of a veterinarian and a behavior/training consultant who may also be the breeder of your Lhasa Apso. Acquiring your Lhasa Apso from a reputable source ought to make this an excellent reserve of information and selecting a veterinarian in advance will supply you with a professional who can answer questions about your Lhasa Apso's health. In the event of illness, never attempt to treat your Lhasa Apso with medications designed for humans. Serious illness or injury always requires veterinary attention so it is best to develop a standing relationship with a veterinarian in case your Lhasa Apso experiences any critical infirmities.

Getting Prepared
Special preparation is required if you have chosen to bring home a puppy or an adult dog. You will need to puppy-proof *all* the areas that your Lhasa Apso will have access to, even if she will be there for only a short

time. Remove or secure things like poisonous household products (plastic bottles can be punctured by tiny
sharp teeth), toxic plants (both inside and outside),
electrical cords, open trash receptacles (ingested alu-
minum foil or a dry sponge can
be fatal), prescription drugs (pick
up any you drop) and human
medications (like aspirin or vitamins). Keep the toilet bowl lid
closed so the inquisitive dog does
not fall in and drown or drink
poisonous bowl cleaner. Water in
buckets, swimming pools and fish
ponds can all be dangerous to the
adult dog as well as to the very
young puppy. Garden sprays, antifreeze and lawn treatments can be
attractive to an inquisitive Lhasa,
but will have deadly results. Objects
small enough to be chewed or swal-
lowed, like needles, pins, staples, marbles, children's
toys, pens or pencils, can cause internal injuries or
obstructions if swallowed. Refer to chapter 7 for further information about ingestion of dangerous products and objects.

*Before you bring
a puppy home,
go through the
house and make
it puppy-safe.*

HOMECOMING

Plan to bring your new Lhasa Apso home during a
weekend or a vacation week specially set aside for
welcoming her into your home. This will give you a
chance to get to know each other and establish a routine that will be compatible to your lifestyle.

If there are small children in your home, be sure to
find out if the new Lhasa Apso has had exposure and
interactions with children. Also evaluate her reaction
to your children. Some Lhasa Apsos like children even
if they have had no experience with them, and others
are not so amiable about little people. After you bring
the Lhasa Apso home, remember that children can
become so enamored with the new pet that they give
her no rest. Make them understand that the new

family member is a living, breathing creature and
needs a break occasionally.

ADJUSTMENT TIME

If you choose an adult Lhasa Apso, she will need to
adjust to her new home, so if possible bring home a
familiar toy, bed or blanket. Having something familiar
from the past will make it easier for the adult Lhasa
Apso to settle into her new home. As you have read
previously, Lhasa Apsos tend to be cautious about
new situations. This does not mean that adults cannot
change homes successfully; however, you will need
to be tolerant of any reluctance to this change until
you are accepted as a new friend. Perhaps a good
comparison is to expect an adult Lhasa Apso to accept her new environment with the same enthusiasm
as a child who comes to visit you and knows no one
in your family.

Although the adult Lhasa Apso usually does not cause
damage by chewing, nor is she inclined to be as curi-
ous as a puppy, until you know her habits it would be
advisable to pet-proof your house much the way you
would for a puppy. Until the adult bonds to your family, special care should be taken so that she does not
escape from your confines as she may try to return to
her previous home.

Winning over or retraining an adult Lhasa Apso can
be a challenge but may be even more rewarding than
training a puppy.

If true to form, upon arriving at her new home one of
the first things your new family member will do is wander around her surroundings. These wanderings
should be allowed yet always supervised in order that
no bad habits develop. Your Lhasa Apso is surveying all
the possibilities for her comfort as well as searching for
a safe place where she can rest or sleep. For your convenience you can choose to make this a roomy but cozy
plastic travel crate with a familiar blanket or bed in it.
This crate can serve as a safe haven for all your Lhasa
Apso's life both at home and when traveling.

Where your Lhasa Apso spends her quiet time is your choice, but keep in mind that your Lhasa Apso will want to be with the family when everyone is home. It is a Lhasa Apso's nature, when allowed, to stay in the same room with her favorite family member. If you have a portable safe haven (such as a crate), she can occasionally spend the night with different family members. However, in the beginning it is advisable to follow a schedule.

Allow your new dog to inspect her new home, but supervise in order to curtail bad habits.

A puppy that is picked from a litter will probably be lonely, especially at night since she has become accustomed to cuddling with her siblings when she sleeps. Whining, howling and crying from loneliness can be very disturbing to her new family. If you have created a safe haven in the form of a travel crate for the new puppy, there are several things that may comfort the unhappy puppy. Setting a clock or radio near the crate or a sturdy stuffed toy that makes soothing noises or plays music in the crate may help the puppy to feel less alone. If you want your Lhasa Apso to always sleep in the area you have designated, do not respond to the puppy's noise. However, if you plan to let her sleep in a family member's room as an adult, it may soothe the puppy to be in the crate in the bedroom with a person that can reach out and comfort her.

A Safe Haven

If your new Lhasa Apso must be alone for more than a few minutes, confine her in a safety-proofed room along with her open crate ("safe haven"), toys and a layer of newspapers on the floor. Never allow your Lhasa Apso, regardless of age, to have unattended access to all of your home until you are sure that her house manners are such that she will not make a mess or hurt herself. Baby gates can be used to confine the Lhasa Apso in a room or a part of the house where she can be with you and yet not wander out of your sight to get into trouble.

Submissive Urination

To prevent escape, make sure your yard is completely secure before allowing your Lhasa outside.

Sometimes puppies urinate when they are excited or nervous. This is involuntary and is the puppy's way of submitting to an experience she feels is threatening or that she does not understand. Usually if this nervous piddling is ignored, the puppy will outgrow it. To scold will make the puppy more nervous and will actually exacerbate the situation.

Collar and Lead

The choice of a collar and lead for your new Lhasa Apso depends on whether she is a puppy or an adult. If the puppy has not worn a collar or been restricted by a leash, you will need to leash train. A narrow leather or cloth collar and lead is a good choice for a Lhasa Apso puppy although a one-piece show lead with an adjustable neck opening also works well. The puppy will first try to scratch this foreign object on her neck, but will soon get accustomed to it. The next step is to use the lead to encourage the puppy to go with you and not fight the restriction. Leash training is well explained in chapter 8 of this book. An adult Lhasa Apso has most likely been trained to walk on lead and, if her hair is clipped short, can wear the collar with an identification tag all the time. When your Lhasa Apso has her natural long hair, continual wearing of a collar causes the hair around the neck to mat. If your Lhasa Apso has long hair, you may wish to identify her with a tattoo or microchip. The American Kennel Club demands that breeders identify each of their dogs, so your Lhasa Apso may be permanently identified when you get her.

It may take your new Lhasa Apso some time to adjust to her new home before she'll be interested in food or water.

FOOD AND WATER

When food and water are first offered to your Lhasa Apso, do not be alarmed if they are refused. Remember that everything is new to your puppy and she is probably worried—food and water are not appealing yet. Continue to offer food and water at the times you have scheduled and your Lhasa Apso will soon relax and eat and drink as she should.

TOYS

Indulge your new puppy or adult Lhasa with toys, but do not allow her to have anything that can be ingested. Soft latex toys are good until holes are chewed in them and the squeaker can be eaten. Stuffed toys are reassuring to the new puppy who has left his cuddly siblings behind; however, if there are any signs of chewing into the stuffing, chewing off plastic nose or eyes or pulling off a neck ribbon take these toys away or only let the puppy have them when you are watching.

OUTDOOR FUN

Before letting your Lhasa Apso loose in your fenced yard, be sure to check for holes that are big enough for her to squeeze through. Lhasa Apsos do not tend to be diggers, but if left to their own devices for long periods of time they may dig in your flower beds or even under the fence.

Remember that whether you choose a puppy or an adult, you have invited a living creature into your home, and your lifestyle has changed. This new family member is entitled to receive your care and protection, in return for which she will give you her unconditional love and loyalty.

chapter 5

Feeding
Your
Lhasa Apso

Because the Lhasa Apso is a small dog, he does not normally have expensive or complicated feeding needs. He does, however, need a well-balanced diet that contains all the nutrients for proper growth, development and maintenance.

Providing the Right Nutritional Balance

There are many kinds of dog foods on the market as well as many opinions about how and when to feed your dog. In order to make an educated decision about what to feed your Lhasa Apso, you will need to understand the "fine print" on the food containers. The *analysis* tells you the percentage of nutrients contained in the food and the *ingredient list* gives you the source of these nutrients. Primary ingredients are listed first with the lesser ingredients listed last.

To be properly fed, your Lhasa Apso should receive the correct types and quantities of the following six nutrients:

1. Proteins
2. Carbohydrates
3. Fats
4. Minerals
5. Vitamins
6. Water

Protein is an essential part of a growing puppy's diet.

PROTEINS

Proteins are a vital part of every living cell whether it is a plant or an animal. They are found not only in the cells but also in the body fluids. Proteins are the chief tissue builders; therefore, the protein needs of puppies are greater than those of the mature Lhasa Apsos. Common protein sources are meat, fish, eggs, gelatin and soybeans; while there are many other sources of protein, they are all made up of amino acids. Certain amino acids are essential, and every dog must get them if he is to live and grow. If a Lhasa Apso receives insufficient amounts of essential amino acids, he can suffer from a protein deficiency even though there may be a high level of total protein in his diet.

CARBOHYDRATES

Carbohydrates are used for fuel by the body. Your Lhasa Apso burns this fuel to keep himself warm and to perform body movements like jumping up to meet you, or tipping his head at a strange sound. Sources of carbohydrates are cereals like wheat, rice, corn and oatmeal. When your Lhasa Apso eats more carbohydrates than he needs, the excess energy may be changed into fat and is stored in the body for future use. If your Lhasa Apso is overweight, it simply means that he has not burned up all the energy supplied by the food he has eaten.

Minerals provide your Lhasa Apso with strong bones and teeth.

FATS

Fats are a concentrated form of nutrients that give about two times as much heat and energy as an equal amount of carbohydrates. Your Lhasa Apso is able to digest rather large amounts of fat, which, within reasonable limits, is good for him because fats provide the essential fatty acids needed for good health. Fats also supply concentrated energy and aid in digestion.

MINERALS

Every Lhasa Apso needs minerals to grow strong bones and teeth, to build blood, to manufacture digestive juices and as a nutrient for every cell structure in the body. Some minerals are highly essential because the dog is unable to manufacture them from any other nutrient. The most important minerals are calcium, phosphorus, sodium and chlorine.

45

VITAMINS

Vitamins interact with other nutrients to keep your dog healthy. For example, the presence of vitamin D makes it possible for your Lhasa Apso to utilize calcium and phosphorus. Without this vitamin, bone formation in growing puppies will cease and a disease called rickets will develop (even though plenty of calcium and phosphorus is contained in the diet). Each vitamin has its own specific function. All of the well-recognized vitamins are required by your Lhasa Apso with the exception of vitamin C, which your Lhasa Apso is able to manufacture within his body.

WATER

Water is so plentiful and easily obtained that its vital importance in nutrition is often overlooked. Your Lhasa Apso's body is about 70 percent water. Without water, he will die more rapidly than from the lack of any other nutrient. He cannot store large supplies of water in his body; *consequently, fresh, clean water must be available at all times.*

Taste Testing

Regardless of how much nutritional value is packed into a dog food, the nutrition will fail if your Lhasa Apso refuses to eat it. The likes and dislikes of dogs are quite different and it is impossible for anyone to determine what a dog will like without consulting the dog. Observation tells us that the dog hears things that we cannot hear and smells things that we cannot smell. From experience we know that dogs may like flavors that do not always appeal to humans; therefore, you may need to offer different dog foods to your Lhasa Apso before you find the one he likes best. Be sure the one he likes is a *nutritionally complete and balanced* dog food.

Dog Foods

Fortunately, dog food manufacturers have done a lot of research to develop excellent commercial dog foods that are nutritionally complete, balanced and palatable. These dog foods are available in three types—dry, semimoist and canned.

DRY FOOD

Dry dog food is easy to store and is less expensive than other types of dog food. It also keeps its freshness longer after opened. Dry dog food has less moisture and is therefore more concentrated and calorically higher than the other two types. Also it helps to maintain healthy teeth and gums because it is brittle and is chewed before it is consumed. Be sure your choice states on the bag that the food is nutritionally complete and balanced.

Do not add items to dry food just because the dry food is unappealing to you. If you are feeding a high-quality nutritionally complete and balanced food there is no reason to add any supplements.

CANNED FOOD

Canned food can be nutritionally complete and balanced but it contains more moisture than other types and therefore provides less calories. You will have to feed three times as much canned food to provide the same calories as dry food. Canned food probably is the most palatable of the three, and a small amount can be used as a flavor additive if your Lhasa Apso does not like plain dry food. Unused canned food must be refrigerated to eliminate spoilage. If you choose to feed canned food, be sure that the label says "nutritionally complete and balanced" because some canned foods are all meat, and meat alone is not a nutritionally complete and balanced diet for your Lhasa Apso.

You may have to offer different types of dog food to your Lhasa before he is satisfied—dogs can be finicky about what they eat.

47

SEMIMOIST FOOD

Semimoist food is conveniently packaged, does not require refrigeration and can be fed alone or added to dry food. This food seems to be quite palatable; however, be sure to provide your dog with enough water because semimoist food may make your Lhasa Apso very thirsty. This author does not recommend semimoist for more than a short-term convenience food or an additive to dry food because it contains an excess of preservatives and color additives.

TIPS

Here are some basic things to consider when choosing a dog food:

- Better quality foods will cost more
- Despite what advertisements say, there is no single food that works for every breed
- Better quality dog foods are usually found at pet supply stores and feed stores

The person from whom you get your new Lhasa Apso will usually recommend that you continue feeding the food that he is presently eating and will provide instructions as to how much and how often to feed. You will usually be provided with a starter bag of food. Continuing with this recommended dog food and feeding schedule is usually a wise decision.

SWITCHING DOG FOOD

Lhasa Apsos may stop eating because of a sudden change in diet. It is best to avoid abruptly changing food brands but if you must change the food, do so gradually over several days. Change food by adding a bit of the new food and increasing the amount added each day until you have gradually changed to the new food.

About Supplements

Never supplement your Lhasa Apso's diet without the recommendation of his breeder or your veterinarian.

Feeding additional vitamins, minerals or even table scraps can disrupt the nutritional balance of your Lhasa Apso's food and can even cause a digestive upset. Before you add dietary extras like cottage cheese, eggs or table scraps to entice your Apso to empty his bowl, remember that no healthy dog is so finicky that he will starve to death with a bowl of fresh food available. If your Apso is a good eater and suddenly stops eating, make an appointment with your veterinarian.

How Much and How Often to Feed

The recommended feeding quantity for small dogs is provided on the bag or label of the dog food you buy for your Lhasa Apso. If your Lhasa Apso eats all the food you give him within twenty minutes and is of the proper weight, you are feeding him the correct amount. If food is left after twenty minutes, you may be overfeeding and will need to offer less food. Usually Lhasa Apso pets tend to be obese rather than too thin, so be sure not to overfeed because obesity is not a healthy condition.

The frequency of meals for your Lhasa Apso depends on his age. Puppies should be eating two to three meals a day and adults one or two meals. Adult Lhasa Apsos do best under specific dietary conditions with protein percentages no higher than 10 percent of their total food consumption. Again, a good quality dog food is the best choice because it will offer a good quality protein. Poor quality protein is not as easily broken down and can put a strain on the kidneys. Lhasa Apsos have a good tolerance for a high-fat diet, containing up to 15 percent of the total diet. Overweight Apsos should be fed food with a lower fat content.

Because puppies have different dietary needs than adults, puppy food is higher in calories, protein and fat—elements necessary for growing bodies. A nutritionally complete and balanced dry puppy food should be fed just as it comes from the bag. Nothing should be added except perhaps a little hot water to release the food's aroma. Puppies up to 6 months old should be fed as much as they will eat in twenty minutes (usually ⅓ to ½ cup) every eight hours. Young puppies fed more frequently may develop loose stools or diarrhea. Whatever is not eaten after twenty minutes should be picked up until the next meal. From 6 months to 1 year of age, the puppy should eat every twelve hours. The amount fed will need to be adjusted as the puppy grows; at 6 months, a Lhasa Apso will eat from ½ to 1 cup of food per feeding. Continue to feed puppy food until your Lhasa Apso is 1 year old.

Some adult Lhasa Apsos tend to have hyperacidity of the stomach. These dogs will often vomit bile or drink a lot of water about twelve hours after their meal because their empty stomachs are secreting too much acid. Apsos with hyperacidity do well if they are fed only half of their meal at one time, followed by the second half twelve hours later. Be sure to stay true to the feeding schedule, as a delay in eating will aggravate the dog's acid levels. If the problem persists after this schedule change, consult your veterinarian.

Evaluating General Health

Although unpleasant, a good way to evaluate your Lhasa Apso's general health and how well his food is being metabolized is to regularly observe his feces. Firm, formed excrement usually means that your Lhasa Apso is eating a high-quality diet that is being utilized by his body and that your Apso is in generally good health. If the feces is soft or has a strange color, this is probably a result of overfeeding or inferior food. Diarrhea or very black stools are signs of health problems and your veterinarian should be consulted.

Food Allergies

Another issue to consider when selecting a dog food is the Lhasa Apso's tendency toward food allergies. Chicken, beef, wheat and corn are the most common antagonists. Although not all Apsos have food allergies and some are allergic to only some of the above foods, the incidence of food allergies is great enough to be cautious. For this reason, you may want to avoid foods where chicken, beef, wheat and corn are listed as primary ingredients. Diets containing lamb and rice as primary ingredients work best and there are several brands available. In the Lhasa Apso's homeland, he ate rice, rye, homemade fat supplements and occasionally a few indigenous insects and carcasses. It is, therefore, not surprising that lamb and rice food is a good choice.

Be aware that Lhasa Apsos tend to be allergic to chicken, beef, wheat and corn.

Bones

Lhasa Apsos like to chew on bones, but any bone that may splinter (like chicken, turkey, pork or lamb) is unsafe and should be disposed of in such a way that your resourceful little Lhasa Apso does not help himself. An ingested bone splinter can cause intestinal trauma and may require surgery. In fact, an impacted or perforated intestine is usually fatal. Round bones, like knucklebones or large leg bones, that do not splinter will make your Lhasa Apso happy and are usually safe. Raw bones are rather pungent and can carry undesirable bacteria, so you should boil them before offering them to your Lhasa Apso. If you have any doubt about the safety of a bone, do not give it to your Lhasa Apso. Many artificial bones are completely safe, and may be safer for your Lhasa than a real bone.

RAWHIDE

There are many opinions about whether rawhide should be considered a safe chewing option. A dog who chews eagerly and actually consumes the bone may ingest enough rawhide to cause a blockage; however, a dog who chews tentatively will probably come to no harm. It is imperative to observe your Lhasa Apso's reaction to the rawhide before giving it to him when he's unattended.

Snack Foods

Remember to remove snacks that could be harmful to your Lhasas, especially during holidays.

Snack foods are fun to feed your Lhasa Apso; however, be sure that these snacks are not given in excess and that they are safe for dogs. Reward your Lhasa Apso only with those treats that have been developed especially for dogs because there are several "danger foods." Chocolate contains two chemicals that are toxic to dogs, caffeine and theobromine. Be particularly careful of where you keep the family treats during holidays, such as Christmas, Halloween and Easter.

Spices used in Italian and Mexican foods can cause severe gastrointestinal upsets and can be deadly for young puppies. Onions are a natural blood thinner—be careful where you store and dispose of this produce. Puppies are the most common offenders as they will chew or eat anything.

Although not harmful in small amounts, excessive amounts of foods normally associated with holidays (such as turkey meat and skin, ham, gravy, mashed potatoes, as well as other table scraps) can cause your Apso to experience an upset stomach and/or a severe case of diarrhea.

Use common sense when choosing your Lhasa Apso's diet, and remember that if you have questions always consult your veterinarian or the breeder.

chapter 6

Grooming
Your
Lhasa Apso

Whether it is the fluffy hair on a puppy or the long, flowing hair gracing an adult, the Lhasa Apso's coat is one of the hallmarks of the breed. You probably appreciate dogs with long hair since you have chosen a Lhasa Apso for a companion. If  you chose your Lhasa Apso because you saw and liked a beautiful dog with a floor-length coat in a photo or at a dog show, please realize that this coat was obtained only by regular and expert grooming. In order for your Apso's coat to become this beautiful, you will need to either take her to a professional grooming shop or develop the expertise to care for her yourself.

Professional Grooming
If you are too busy or do not wish to do the grooming, find a professional groomer who understands and likes Lhasa Apsos, and who

has experience grooming them. Set up a schedule so that your Lhasa Apso is groomed regularly. Depending on the type of coat and the environment you live in, this schedule can range from a weekly appointment to a monthly bath (with you doing upkeep grooming in between visits to the groomer).

Grooming at Home

Read on if you have decided to groom your Lhasa Apso yourself. Grooming is quite easy if done correctly and can be fun and relaxing for both you and your Lhasa Apso. With the proper tools, patience, common sense and the instructions from this book, you can have a beautifully groomed Apso by spending only a few hours grooming her each week.

Supplies

Some of the tools and products needed to groom your Lhasa Apso include the following:

- Cushioned pin brush with flexible metal pins or a combination natural bristle and nylon pin brush
- Curved slicker brush
- Soft toothbrush and canine eye wash solution
- Hemostat and cotton swabs or cotton-tipped sticks
- Toenail clippers and styptic powder
- Blunt-end scissors
- Knitting needle or rattail comb
- Plastic bottle with fine spray applicator
- Hands-free hair dryer
- Small latex bands and barrettes
- Canine shampoo that is recommend for long-haired breeds
- Flea and tick shampoo or rinse that is recommend for longhaired breeds
- Conditioner or creme rinse

These tools and grooming products can usually be purchased from a well-stocked dog supply shop or from a vendor at dog shows.

Training Your Lhasa to Accept Grooming

Grooming can be enjoyable if your Lhasa Apso is trained to allow you to groom her without a struggle. This training should start as early as possible. One of the first things a Lhasa Apso puppy should learn is to lie quietly on her side on a flat grooming surface.

The correct way to teach a Lhasa Apso to lay on her side is to first stand her sideways in front of you on the grooming surface. Next, grasp the front and back legs on her opposite side, lift her slightly, and push her over and away from your body. At the same time, lean over your Lhasa Apso while holding her and speaking softly until she relaxes. Then gently and slowly slip your hands and body away and at the same time give a verbal "stay" command until your Lhasa Apso lays still without being held. If she struggles and stands up, repeat this exercise until you have convinced her that lying on her side is okay, will not harm her and is not dangerous. Practice laying your Apso on her side until she will stay there without being held, thus freeing your hands for grooming. When you have finished a practice session, praise and reward your Lhasa Apso for having pleased you.

Allow your Lhasa Apso to relieve herself before you start grooming to avoid restlessness. Also give her a break occasionally if her coat condition requires a long grooming session.

A grooming table, or other flat surface will make grooming easy. You can use any surface that you are comfortable either standing or sitting beside—if you are uncomfortable, you will tend to rush and your grooming will be less thorough. Never groom your Apso on the floor or on your bed because you will be uncomfortable, your Apso will have the advantage of being on a surface she usually plays or runs on and the grooming results will be disappointing. Portable, folding grooming tables of different or adjustable heights are available and would be a sensible investment.

A Lhasa Apso puppy's coat mats very little the first few months of her life and thus grooming sessions for a young puppy are really for the purpose of training her to lie still. By the time the coat changes (when it starts matting-tangling) at 6 to 9 months, your Lhasa Apso will be trained to lie still while you brush.

Let the Grooming Begin

When your Lhasa Apso has learned to lie down without struggling or getting up, the real grooming process begins. Before actually brushing the hair, spray it with

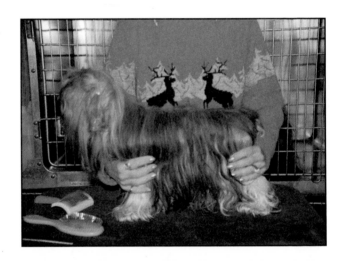

The first step to teaching your Lhasa to lay on her side is to stand her sideways in front of you.

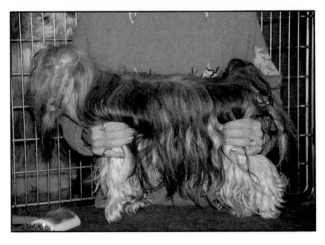

Next, grasp the front and back legs on the dog's opposite side, lift her slightly and gently push her over and away from you.

a fine mist of water or a commercial coat spray or conditioner. This will help to lubricate the dry coat, protect the ends and help control the static electricity, thus making the coat more manageable.

Start brushing by first pushing all the hair away from you and exposing the skin of the stomach. Having a starting point helps to avoid getting the hair caught in your brush or comb and allows you to see the area to be groomed. The exposed skin of the stomach should form a horizontal part in the hair. The part need not be perfectly straight, but if you do not make a part, you

Once she's on her side, speak softly to her until she relaxes.

Slip your hands from under the dog and give her the Stay command until she lays still without being held.

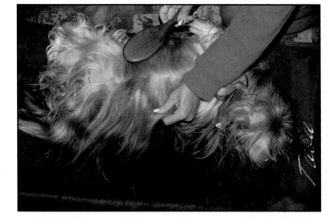

Make your starting point with a horizontal part in the hair covering your Lhasa's stomach.

Keep the brush flat on the hair and brush a small amount of hair at a time.

may not be grooming the hair all the way down to the skin or you may miss some areas entirely.

After spraying the coat, use the pin or bristle/nylon combination brush to brush a small portion of hair down toward the grooming surface. Continue brushing horizontally from the front to the back of the body. Take care to brush only a small amount of hair, thus moving the part a fraction of an inch up the side of the body. Keep the brush flat on the hair, avoiding any twisting, turning or flipping action which tends to break the ends of the hair.

After moving the part up about an inch with the brush, use the medium tooth side of the steel comb on the same area making sure that there are no tangles or mats that were missed with the brush. Do not flip, twist or turn the comb—simply pull it gently straight through the hair. If the comb is stopped by a snarl, just lift it straight up and out of the hair and start over very gently, working the tangle to within a few inches of the ends of the hair. Use the brush to gently work the snarl out the last few inches. Continue this inch-by-inch grooming procedure until you have groomed the entire body on both sides of your Lhasa Apso, including her chest and rear.

If you discover a mat too large to work out with the comb or brush, use your fingers to spread the mat apart. After separating the mat with your fingers use the brush to work out the mat. Plenty of patience is a definite asset when working out mats. The more you separate the mat into smaller mats or tangles the less damage you will cause to the hair.

Another way to remove a large mat is to use the corner of the slicker brush in a "picking" action gently pulling hair bit by bit from the mat.

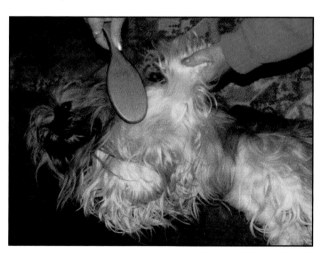

Hold the leg and most of the leg hair back when grooming each leg.

LEGS

Grooming the legs requires you to hold the foot and most of the leg hair at the same time. Start at the base of the leg next to the body. Brush the hair away from the foot and toward the body. By following the same technique as you did on the body, the part should appear completely around the leg. Brush the leg until you have reached the foot. After all the leg hair has been completely brushed and detangled, lightly brush the coat downward toward the foot so that it falls in its natural direction. The hair under your Lhasa Apso's legs closest to the body tends to mat quickly, so be sure to get all the tangles from this area. Be very gentle—this is one of the most sensitive areas to groom.

Part the hair on the tail, then spray and brush the hair on either side of the part.

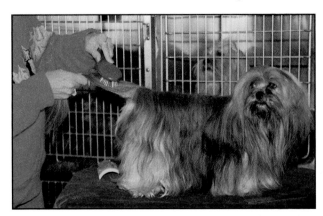

TAIL

The tail should be groomed by taking all the tail hair from the base of the tail to its end and making a part down one side. Fold all the hair over to one side and spray and brush. After brushing the tail, comb to check for tangles.

HEAD

The head is groomed the same as the body by using the part, brush and comb method. Be sure to groom under the chin and neck as well.

The facial area requires special attention and more frequent grooming because food particles may adhere to the hair around the mouth, and matter accumulates under the eyes. Brush the ends of the beard carefully to avoid scratching the eyes, lips or nose. After brushing and combing the beard and whiskers thoroughly, use the fine tooth part of the steel comb close to the eyes to pull the hair gently away from each eye. Repeat this until all of the eye matter is removed with the comb. If the eye matter has dried, use a wet cotton swab to moisten it before combing. A soft toothbrush is also a good tool for cleaning this area. Two drops of eye wash solution in each eye will help to rinse away any matter in the eyes. Cleaning this facial area frequently will help to eliminate a buildup of eye matter or food particles and will aid in eliminating odor, infection and a generally untidy appearance.

Use a steel comb to gently groom the facial hair.

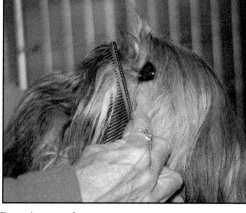

Trimming the hair under the eyes or on the muzzle is not recommended because it may result in an irritation to the eyes, especially as it grows out. The hair under the eyes, if allowed to grow long enough, will drape down the side of the muzzle and will not irritate the eyes. Puppies can have excessive tearing until their hair has grown long enough to drape down the side of the muzzle and away from the eyes. During this time the puppy's eyes should be cleaned often.

EARS

Another area that might need special attention between regular grooming sessions is the ears. They can become sticky from dragging in the food bowl. It may be necessary to spray their ends until wet and to gently brush them to remove the residue. After brushing the ears, gently comb to be sure no tangles have been missed. Be careful not to scratch the ear leather or damage the hair ends with the teeth of the comb.

Because the Lhasa Apso is a long-coated dog, she has hair in her ears. This hair should be removed periodically, particularly if the ear shows signs of odor, debris or infection. To remove the hair from inside the ears first lay your Lhasa Apso on her side. Next hold the ear leather with one hand, exposing the ear canal, and with the other hand use either your thumb and forefinger or a hemostat to pull a few hairs at a time until the ear canal is free from hair. Always use a steady pull and do not jerk or pull too much hair at one time. Only pull the hair that is long enough to grasp, and do not probe deeply into the ear. Applying ear powder before pulling the hair makes it easier to pull. This powder is available at most pet supply shops.

After the hair has been removed put several drops of ear cleaner or mineral oil in the ear. Using cotton swabs or pieces of cotton placed on the end of the hemostat, swab the ear until it is dry. Do not to probe deeply into the ear. Let your Apso stand up and shake, then swab the ear again. Repeat the whole procedure if the cotton is stained brown on the last swabbing. If this brown stain on the cotton persists after the ears have been cleaned several times, it would be best to check with your veterinarian. The ears should be cleaned each time your Lhasa Apso is groomed.

CLIPPING TOENAILS

Clip your Lhasa Apso's toenails frequently enough to keep the nails short. The nails should never be allowed to grow long enough to absorb the pressure of walking, as this is uncomfortable for your Lhasa Apso. To clip the nails, lay your Lhasa Apso on her side and grasp one foot in your hand. Use your index finger to push the hair away from the nails and place your thumb between the pads. With the nail clipper in your other hand, clip the tip off of the nail a little at a time until the blunt end of the nail appears pink on a light-colored nail or moist on a black nail. If you clip off too much of the nail it will bleed. Stop any bleeding by immediately applying styptic powder and pressure to the end of the nail.

Your Lhasa Apso should have the hair between her pads trimmed monthly. Do this by first laying your Apso

on her side, then using the blunt-end scissors to trim
the excess hair that has grown between the pads. Be
careful not to trim so close as to cut the skin. If the hair
on top of the feet grows so long as to be a nuisance, it
can be trimmed into a round, neat appearance.

ANAL AND GENITAL AREAS

Your Lhasa Apso's long hair can cause the area around
her genitals or anus to be soiled. These areas should
be cleaned as a part of regular grooming. Between
grooming sessions, clean as often as needed by spraying until wet, sprinkling on baby powder and brushing
until fairly dry. Reapply the powder if needed. The
powder helps to absorb moisture, remove stains and
control odor. If your Lhasa Apso is too messy in either
area, bathe her. The hair growing around the anus
should be trimmed to eliminate the collection of fecal
material. Check each time your Lhasa Apso eliminates
for any fecal matter that may have adhered to her coat.
Lhasa Apsos often report such problems to their family because they really do not like to be untidy.

When your Lhasa Apso has been thoroughly brushed;
her ears, eyes and genitals cleaned; and her toenails,
pads and feet trimmed, she is ready to have her hair
parted from the tip of her nose to the base of her tail
and to have her head hair fastened back from her eyes.

Parting the Hair

When having her hair parted, your Lhasa Apso should
be standing four square and facing you so that the part
can be centered and straight. Use the knitting needle
or rattail comb to make the part down the back. Starting at the center of the nose, between the eyes and over
the skull, the part should aim for the base of the tail and
following the spinal column to center the part. Spray
the part lightly and brush the hair straight down on
both sides of the body.

TOPKNOTS

After your Apso has been parted from nose to tail it is
time to determine if she has enough headfall for one

or two topknots. The longer, thicker headfall requires two topknots, while a shorter headfall will stay up better with one. If you use one topknot, make a part from the outer corner of each eye to the back of the skull just above the ears. Do not make the part below the eyes or ears because this will be uncomfortable and your Lhasa Apso will ruin the topknot by scratching or rubbing. Next, brush the two portions of hair straight back from the face to the top of the head mak-

ing one strand or ponytail of hair. Secure this strand of hair with a latex band or barrette.

When using two topknots, follow the same procedure except leave the portions on each side of the part separate. Secure each ponytail just above the ear and allow the hair to hang over the ear. Be careful not to catch any hair from the ears in the latex band or barrette because this will cause irritation and your Lhasa Apso will destroy your work by scratching or rubbing. Either style of topknot should be retied several times a week. Do not secure the topknots too tightly or allow them to remain up for more than one week because matting and skin irritation can result. Another way to fasten your Apso's headfall away from her face is to braid the sections of hair and secure the end of the braid with a latex band. When introducing your Lhasa Apso to a topknot, divert her attention from the strange new thing on her head by taking her for a ride in the car or a walk in the park.

Bathing

Your Lhasa Apso should be bathed as often as is needed to keep her clean. The frequency of bathing will depend upon the environment in which she lives. A Lhasa Apso who exercises on a concrete or gravel patio will need less bathing than one who is walked on oily city streets.

Prepare your Lhasa Apso for her bath by performing a regular grooming as previously described. With all mats and tangles removed, place her in a sink or bath-tub (leaving the drain open). Using a spray attachment or dipping container, completely saturate the coat. Be careful not to get water in the ears. Apply a shampoo to the coat that is recommended for longhaired dogs, and be careful not to get it in the eyes. You may wish to use a tearless shampoo for the head and around the eyes. Do not rub the shampoo into the coat. Squeeze it in as you would when hand washing a delicate gar-ment. Rinse the shampoo out of the coat and apply shampoo again if needed. Always rinse *all* the sham-poo out of the coat, otherwise skin irritation may result. Applying a creme rinse or conditioner accord-ing to directions will make brushing tangles from the wet coat easier, but will not demat a coat. Dematting should be done before the bath because getting mats wet makes them tighter and harder to remove.

FLEA AND TICK RINSES

If there are any fleas or ticks on your Lhasa Apso, use a flea or tick rinse. Be sure to accurately follow mix-ing directions to avoid irritation or illness by applying an overly strong mixture. Conversely, an overly weak mixture will not effectively eliminate the fleas and ticks. Ask your veterinarian to recommend a flea and tick rinse. This rinse need not have an offensive odor and may be used to prevent attracting fleas or ticks if you anticipate bringing your Lhasa Apso to a location such as a park or wooded area. Use a flea and tick rinse only as needed and not routinely after every bath.

DRYING YOUR LHASA

After the rinses have been applied and your Lhasa Apso is ready to be dried, first wrap her in a large terry-cloth towel to absorb all excess moisture. You may need to use two towels, but never rub your Lhasa Apso with the towel to dry her because this will create tan-gles and mats that are difficult to remove.

Next, remove the towel and lay your Lhasa Apso on her side on the grooming surface. Turn the hair dryer on warm and direct it toward your Lhasa Apso's stomach. Start to brush as you dry and follow the method used in general grooming, by forming the horizontal parting of the coat and brushing until dry down to the skin. After your Lhasa Apso is dry, put the finishing touches on her by parting her from nose to tail and securing her headfall.

Be patient at all times during grooming sessions. With practice your expertise will increase, and if you groom your Lhasa Apso regularly and thoroughly, she will not only have a beautiful coat but will also be a healthier, happier pet.

Different Styles
THE SHORT PET CLIP

If you have difficulty keeping your Lhasa Apso properly groomed or live in an area where her coat picks up an excess of debris, you may need to keep the coat in a short pet clip. Any professional grooming shop that has experience with Lhasa Apsos can give your Apso the hair style that suits her, or you can learn to clip her yourself.

THE SCHNAUZER CLIP

If you do not want to cope with your dog's long coat, a serviceable style for your Apso can be created by using an electric clipper to clip the hair on the head, neck, back and sides short, leaving the leg hair slightly longer. Trim the tail, ears, beard and whiskers with scissors to make her look neat. This clip, commonly called a Schnauzer clip, is attractive and is easier to maintain than a longer coat.

A NECESSITY CLIP

Another style is to clip or trim all the hair on the back, legs and feet to the same length and blend it with the longer head hair by trimming the head hair shorter.

If you walk with your Lhasa Apso in fields and woods where sticks, leaves and brambles get caught in her long coat, you may choose to completely clip your Lhasa Apso from head to tail in varying lengths according to the season. A necessity clip should be performed if you have allowed your Apso to become overly matted. It is much better for an Apso to have her hair clipped off than to attempt to brush an extremely matted coat. Even when it is possible to do so, dematting can be painful and will result in a thin, straggly and unkempt looking coat.

Providing routine grooming, either by yourself or a professional groomer, will keep your Lhasa Apso looking attractive whether you choose to clip her or to keep her in her natural long coat.

chapter 7

Keeping Your
Lhasa Apso
Healthy

Lhasa Apsos, in general, are hardy and have few genetic or congenital tendencies for disease and debilitation. This hardiness is probably the result of the Apso's development in the challenging environment of Tibet. They do, however, still need the services of a veterinarian if it is only for proper preventive care. Your Lhasa Apso will probably never experience most of the health concerns explained in this chapter; however, they are included to alert you to possible symptoms to watch for.

Selecting a Veterinarian

The selection of a veterinarian is one of the most important decisions you will make for your Lhasa Apso because you will be relying on his or her expertise for many years to help keep your Apso healthy. Ask friends, neighbors or breeders for recommendations, and do not hesitate to visit more than one

Your veterinarian should understand the Lhasa Apso's unique behavior and health needs.

veterinarian until you are comfortable with his or her credentials and manner. Do understand, however, that you are responsible for knowing as much as possible about your Apso in order that you can accurately answer any questions the veterinarian asks about your dog. Accurate information about your Apso's condition is very important in making a diagnosis.

Some criteria to consider when choosing a veterinarian are:

- Must have an understanding of Lhasa Apso temperament and is not affronted by the Apso's sentinel behavior

- Must be knowledgeable about the breed's health needs

- Must know how to treat breed-specific conditions

- Accessible for after-hour emergencies and consultations

- Has a competent staff

- Conveniently located

- Office hours coincide with your schedule

- Able to explain information to you in terms you can understand

Living with
a Lhasa Apso

Preventive Care

Preventive care is the best way to keep your Lhasa Apso healthy. Immunizing puppies and providing yearly booster shots for adults is an important part

Check your dog's teeth frequently and brush them regularly.

of preventive care as are proper nourishment, routine stool checks for internal parasites, keeping ears, eyes and teeth clean, routine grooming and external parasitic prevention.

VACCINES

The following immunizations will help prevent diseases that are harmful to your Lhasa's health.

Make sure that your puppy gets all of his shots at the right times, and have him neutered, too. These are both preventive measures that will keep your Lhasa in top health.

Distemper Distemper is a highly contagious viral disease that causes fever, discharge from eyes and nose, coughing, vomiting, diarrhea, lethargy, seizures and finally death. Patients that appear to have been successfully treated can later develop undesirable problems like convulsions, muscle twitches, lack of coordination and even paralysis. Because there seems to be no particular cure, and treatment is not usually successful, it is crucial that your Lhasa Apso be immunized against this disease and that he receives an annual booster vaccination.

Hepatitis Hepatitis is a viral disease, is contagious and can affect dogs of all ages but is most serious in puppies. It affects the liver and has symptoms including fever, vomiting, abdominal pain and bloody diarrhea. The canine form of hepatitis is not the same disease that affects humans and can only be transmitted from dog to dog. Immunize your Apso annually to prevent this disease.

70

Leptospirosis Leptospirosis is a bacterial disease that can also affect humans. Symptoms include fever, vomiting, depression, bloody diarrhea, jaundice and abdominal pain. Yearly booster shots will prevent your Apso from contracting this disease.

Parainfluenza Parainfluenza is a virus that contributes to infectious tracheobronchitis, commonly known as "kennel cough," which is highly contagious and characterized by a hacking cough and gagging. Affected dogs usually do not stop eating but prolonged coughing can develop into more serious problems. This virus is controlled by annual inoculations.

Parvovirus Parvovirus is a viral disease that affects the intestinal tract of dogs. Any unvaccinated canine is susceptible, although young puppies are most seriously affected. The first symptoms of parvovirus infection are listlessness and loss of appetite followed by vomiting and a profuse, waterlike and bloody diarrhea. These symptoms (particularly in puppies) can cause severe dehydration. Puppies that are vaccinated for parvovirus are protected from this disease in most cases. Your Apso should receive a yearly booster shot to protect him against this virus.

Coronavirus Infection Coronavirus infection is difficult to differentiate from parvovirus because of similar symptoms like foul smelling, bloody, waterlike diarrhea. Dogs usually become very dehydrated and if untreated, coronavirus can be fatal. Your Apso should be vaccinated to protect him against this virus.

Rabies Rabies is a fatal viral disease that attacks the central nervous system. This disease can be contracted by dogs that come in contact with the saliva of infected warm-blooded animals—usually wild animals. Rabies can be passed on to humans. There is no effective treatment for rabies after the onset of clinical signs in dogs or man. In dogs, the signs are paralysis of the jaw muscles and throat, inability to swallow, profuse salivation, irritability and extreme aggression. Because rabies is almost always fatal it is very important to inoculate your Lhasa Apso against this disease in order to protect your family, your Apso and the community. Vaccination is advised every one to three years depending upon the type of vaccine used and state law requirements.

Whether you have chosen an adult or a puppy Lhasa Apso, your new pet should have received the pertinent vaccinations before being taken home. If you find yourself accepting a puppy or an adult without up-to-date vaccinations, it is imperative that he be seen by a veterinarian immediately. Additionally, it is recommended that your new Apso be seen by your veterinarian during the first few days of ownership to verify his good health and, in the case of a puppy, to continue his vaccination schedule. Most veterinarians will have you return several times for repeat vaccinations to insure that your Apso puppy is properly protected against disease.

PUPPY'S VACCINE SCHEDULE

Your puppy's vaccine schedule will vary depending on the age, previous vaccine history, and the possibility of exposure to contagious disease. In general a puppy should be vaccinated at 6 weeks, 9 weeks, 12 weeks (at which time leptospirosis is included in the vaccine) and 15 weeks of age. Some veterinarians may encourage another vaccine at 18 weeks. A final parvovirus vaccine should be administered after 20 weeks of age. By law, in most states, any dog over 6 months of age must be vaccinated for rabies, however, the rabies vaccine itself can be administered to a puppy as young as 14 weeks. Vaccines can be administered only to healthy puppies, not sickly ones and, most importantly, puppies unaffected by the very diseases contained in the vaccine.

> **YOUR PUPPY'S VACCINES**
>
> Vaccines are given to prevent your dog from getting an infectious disease like canine distemper or rabies. Vaccines are the ultimate preventive medicine: They're given before your dog ever gets the disease so as to protect him from the disease. That's why it is necessary for your dog to be vaccinated routinely. Puppy vaccines start at 8 weeks of age for the five-in-one DHLPP vaccine and are given every three to four weeks until the puppy is 16 months old. Your veterinarian will put your puppy on a proper schedule and will remind you when to bring in your dog for shots.

The incidence of vaccine failure in puppies has recently been discovered to be on the rise in the Lhasa

Apso breed. That is, the immune system in a few puppies fails to properly develop a resistance to distemper, adenovirus, parvovirus and the other diseases present in the vaccine. Sickness is not caused by the vaccine but rather the body's failure to protect itself when exposed to an outside source. Immune suppression can be the result of familial genetic tendencies or brought on by stress. For added protection, Lhasa Apso puppies should not go to new homes until they are at least 12 weeks old and have had at least two vaccines.

Signs of Illness

Recognizing the signs of illness will promptly help your veterinarian diagnose the problem and improve the possibility of a good prognosis. A list follows of symptoms that should alert you that something is wrong with your Apso. If any of the signs persist for more than twelve to twenty-four hours—consult your veterinarian.

- Vomiting and/or diarrhea
- Increases or decreases in food and/or water intake
- Abnormal behavior—withdrawn, listless, lethargic, depressed
- Elevated temperature—higher than 103°F
- Frequent urination, straining to urinate and/or blood in urine
- Apparent pain and/or sensitivity to touch
- Runny nose and/or eyes
- Coughing and/or choking
- Shallow and/or strained breathing
- Bloat (immediately contact your veterinarian)
- Limping
- Swelling and/or lumps
- Discharge from vulva or penis
- Back and/or neck pain

How to Take Your Dog's Temperature

Because an elevated temperature is one of the first signs of an infection, it is important to know how to properly assess your Lhasa Apso's temperature. The normal temperature for a Lhasa Apso is between 100° and 101°F. To accurately determine your Lhasa Apso's temperature you must use a rectal thermometer. Here are the steps to follow:

1. Shake the thermometer down to below 95°F.

2. Lubricate the thermometer with petroleum jelly.

3. Stand your Lhasa Apso on the grooming surface and gently insert the thermometer into his anus, making sure your Apso does not sit down.

4. Hold the thermometer in place for several minutes.

5. Remove the thermometer, clean it with a tissue and read it.

6. Before putting the thermometer away, be sure to clean it with an alcohol swab.

Internal Parasites

There are several internal parasites specific to dogs. The most commonly seen are roundworms, hookworms, tapeworms, whipworms, heartworms, coccidia and giardia. Roundworms, hookworms, whipworms and heartworms are all from a family of parasites known as ascarids.

Roundworms

Roundworm infestation is common because the worms are passed from the mother to the puppies through the placenta prior to birth. This causes the puppies to be born infested. Roundworms are also transmitted to the puppy through the mother's milk. This permits a chronic exposure to the parasite in the first weeks of the puppy's life. Adult worms live off of food substances that are passed through the digestive tract.

Roundworms also can invade a puppy's body through oral ingestion of egg-laden soil or stool. The larvae go through an intricate migration through the viscera involving the intestinal tract, surrounding tissues, lungs, trachea and stomach. The journey from the trachea and back into the intestines is accomplished by coughing, a classic symptom in roundworm infested puppies. Other symptoms include weight loss, diarrhea, potbellied appearance, lethargy, stunted growth and spaghettilike worms in the stool. While traveling through the tissues, some of the migrating larvae encyst in the tissues and remain there. In the male dog, they stay dormant but in the female, the larvae emerge from their encysted state the last week of pregnancy and migrate through the tissues, through the placenta and directly into the puppies. It is also the emerging larvae that cause milk-borne infestation through transmammary migration. Eggs appear in the puppy's stool at 3 weeks of age.

You'll want to run your hands over your Apso's body every day to check for cuts, parasites or anything unusual on his skin.

Roundworms can be contracted by humans by ingesting their eggs. In people, the worm will grow only into the larval stage. Although the larvae can migrate into human tissues, this is very rare. Nonetheless, because of the danger of infestation, puppies with roundworms are considered a public health hazard. A puppy should be appropriately wormed and should have a "clear" fecal test before he is allowed to enter a home with children.

HOOKWORMS

Hookworms are the second most common ascarid parasite seen in dogs. Hookworms, like roundworms, live in the small intestine. They are bloodsuckers, "hooking" their mouths into the inner lining of the intestine and feeding directly off of their host's bloodstream.

Symptoms include weight loss, anemia, pallor, tarry or blood-tinged stool and bloody diarrhea. Hookworm infestation occurs through the same means as a round-worm infestation. Hookworm larvae also can enter the body directly through the skin, a condition known as cutaneous larval migrans. Eggs appear in the stool three weeks after infestation.

WHIPWORMS

Whipworms are the hardest ascarid to diagnose because they live in the cecum or the appendix of the

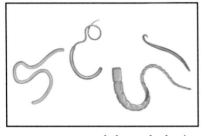

Common internal parasites (l-r): roundworm, whipworm, tapeworm and hookworm.

dog and shed eggs erratically, making it difficult to find them in a stool sample. Subsequently, this parasite is also the hardest to eradicate because medication does not enter the cecum easily. Infestation occurs as a result of direct ingestion. The larvae travel through the intestines until they reach the cecum. Here they embed into the mucosa and feed off of the host's blood and tissue fluids. Symptoms are bright blood streaking in the stool, mucoid stool and occasional diarrhea. Whipworms are probably the least taxing ascarid for the body because of their isolated location in the small intestine. Once shed in the stool, the infectious eggs survive up to five years in the soil.

TAPEWORMS

Tapeworms are a different type of parasite called cestode. Their eggs are shed not individually, like the ascarids, but in segments or proglottids, which pass directly from the intestines or in the stool. Of all the parasites, tapeworms are the least taxing on their host. Infestation occurs as a result of ingestion of an intermediate host, most commonly fleas. Thus, dogs infested with fleas will most likely have tapeworms as well. Infestation can also be caused by access to an animal that has eaten an egg-laden segment or by ingesting raw sheep, rodent or rabbit tissue. Clinical signs may include a dry coat and slight thinness but the most common symptom is the presence of ricelike tape-worm segments in the stool. The segments can also become lodged in the hair around the anus and their migration in this area will sometimes induce itching. Medications effective against ascarids do not serve as a remedy for all species of tapeworms.

GIARDIA

Giardia are protozoan parasites. Giardia eggs or oocysts show up in concentrated populations where the protozoa contaminate food and water sources and survive while waiting to be eaten by their next host. Wild animals are a chronic source of infection. Giardia interferes with intestinal absorption of food which leads to light-colored, foul-smelling diarrhea and weight loss. Adult dogs often carry the parasite in numbers too low to cause symptoms—their healthy immune systems keep the population in check. However, in puppies, the stresses of viral and bacterial infections or other parasites will cause the opportunistic giardia to increase their population.

COCCIDIA

Coccidia, like giardia, are a protozoan parasite that infects a dog by direct ingestion of the oocysts, ingestion of infected intermediate hosts (such as rodents), and ingestion of infected raw meat. Most infestations rarely cause clinical symptoms, but in cases of immuno-suppression, overcrowded conditions and other high-stress situations, signs can include vomiting, mucoid to bloody diarrhea, weight loss and dehydration. As with giardia, adult dogs often carry the parasite in numbers too low to cause symptoms—their stable immune systems keep the population under control.

Though some mild diarrhea cases in newly acquired puppies are harmless, preventing coccidia and giardia infections are good reasons for such puppies to see a veterinarian. A healthy puppy, wormed at the appropriate age and parasite free at the time of purchase, could still "break" with a protozoan infection while adjusting to his new environment.

An annual fecal check by your veterinarian is a necessity because not all intestinal parasites are visible with the naked eye. Also, certain areas of the western and southern United States have additional parasites specific to their environment that are capable of infesting a dog. If you live in these areas, your local veterinarian can assist in determining if these parasites are of concern.

Never attempt to treat your Apso with over-the-counter wormers or herbal remedies. Effective diagnosis and treatment of intestinal parasites is accomplished by a microscopic exam followed by treatment with appropriate prescription medications. No single worming medication is effective for all intestinal parasites and some can even be harmful in the presence of certain parasites or diseases. Consult your veterinarian.

HEARTWORMS

Heartworms are ascarids that invade the pulmonary arteries and, in severe cases, the right atrium of the heart and the vena cava. They are transmitted in the following manner: A female mosquito bites an infected dog; the larvae go through further development in the mosquito for about two weeks; the mosquito deposits the heartworm larvae into another dog during a blood meal; the larvae migrate through the tissues and arrive in the bloodstream about three months later and into the heart about two months later. Microfilaria, "baby heartworms," can be detected in the bloodstream about six months after infection. Though indigenous to tropical and subtropical climates, heartworm infections occur with enough frequency in northern areas to require protection. Heartworm is one parasite best prevented—do not wait to treat an infestation. Several types of heartworm prevention drugs are available through your veterinarian, some eradicate other parasites in addition to heartworm. Annual testing is recommended for all dogs.

Clinical signs of adult worm infestation include exercise intolerance, cough and labored breathing. Severe infestations can cause other complications and conditions, turning heartworm infestation into heartworm disease. The presence of microfilaria and/or heartworm antigens in the bloodstream indicate an infection. Blood tests for heartworm are available through your veterinarian.

Treatment of heartworm disease involves first eliminating the adult worms and then the microfilaria. This treatment is costly to the owner and physically taxing to the patient, sometimes causing complications even in good patient candidates (dogs that are not elderly or otherwise in ill health).

External Parasites

External parasites are usually irritating to your Lhasa Apso. They can invade your Apso in various ways with different results. The following are some external parasites that can affect your Apso.

FLEAS

Fleas manage to find any breed of dog and Lhasa Apsos are not exempt. A rule of thumb is "if you find one, there are ten more hiding." Due to the Apso's dense coat, fleas can often go undetected until the infestation is high. An infested dog will also mean an infested house and yard, as the fleas will often jump off the dog after a meal and lay eggs in

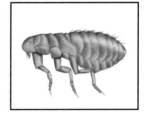

The flea is a die-hard pest.

the dog's habitat. These eggs hatch and continue the life cycle. Clinical signs include intense itching. Even if the insects themselves go undetected, evidence of their presence include tiny red bite lesions on the skin, thinning hair from scratching, and blackened sugar-size granules in the hair. The granules are actually flea excrement and when placed on a wet paper towel, dissolve into a red stain. Treatment must include not only the Apso but his environment and must be repeated often enough to break the flea's three-week life cycle.

Living with
a Lhasa Apso

Insecticide shampoo is the most common combat against fleas. Several topical "spot" treatments are available as are oral prescription products. Flea collars are not generally recommended for Lhasa Apsos because they fail to give full body protection and will cause the hair around the neck to mat. Beware of certain flea "dips" or rinses that can leave an insecticide residual requiring veterinary treatment. Beware of excessive use of one flea-killing chemical or combining one chemical with another, which can cause illness, even death. Always consult your veterinarian for the safest and most effective insecticides for both treating your Apso and his surroundings.

FIGHTING FLEAS

Remember, the fleas you see on your dog are only part of the problem—the smallest part! To rid your dog and home of fleas, you need to treat your dog *and* your home. Here's how:

• Identify where your pet(s) sleep. These are "hot spots."

• Clean your pets' bedding regularly by vacuuming and washing.

• Spray "hot spots" with a non-toxic, long-lasting flea larvicide.

• Treat outdoor "hot spots" with insecticide.

• Kill eggs on pets with a product containing insect growth regulators (IGRs).

• Kill fleas on pets per your veterinarian's recommendation.

TICKS

Ticks are usually active in warm weather and are normally found in tall grass or wooded areas. Ticks feed on blood by attaching their mouths to a warm-blooded animal including humans. Although ticks are distasteful to the owner, an occasional tick does not seem to irritate a Lhasa Apso. In excess, ticks can cause anemia; however, regular grooming will help you to find any that have attached themselves to your Apso. To remove a tick, first spray with a small amount of flea/tick spray or put a drop of alcohol on it so that it will relax its hold. After a few minutes, remove the tick by grasping its head close to the skin with tweezers and pulling it off. Be careful not to leave the head of the tick embedded in your Apso's skin. After removing the tick use an antibiotic spray or ointment to prevent infection.

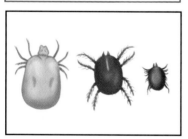

Three types of ticks (l-r): the wood tick, brown dog tick and deer tick.

Lyme Disease

Lyme disease is associated with the bite of an infected deer tick. Both dogs and people can contract this disease by being bitten by an infected tick, but the disease cannot be passed from dog to humans. Consult your veterinarian about the advantages of a vaccination to prevent Lyme disease for your Apso.

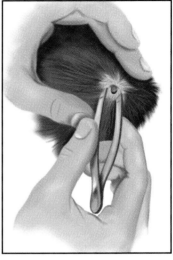

Use tweezers to remove ticks from your dog.

DEMODECTIC MANGE

Demodectic mange, or demodex, is caused by a cigar-shaped mite that lives in the hair follicles. This condition is very rare in Lhasa Apsos. The demodex mite commonly exists in low populations on most canines, but its numbers can flare during stressful periods (especially on a puppy). Disease and immunosuppressive conditions will open the door for a mite population increase. Puppies requiring treatment are often born to mothers who carry the mites. Clinical signs include patches of hair loss, a red rash (demodex is also called "red mange") and intense itching. The rash can be so severe that the dog develops secondary staph infections. Diagnosis is accomplished by collecting skin cells with a procedure called "skin scraping" and looking for the mites under the microscope. Treatment can be accomplished with oral prescription medication in mild cases, or topical treatments over several weeks for more severe infestations.

SARCOPTIC MANGE

Sarcoptic mange, or scabies, is found in many species and can be passed from one species to another. Scabies, too, is rare in Lhasa Apsos, but other animals (even humans) infected with this mite can transmit it to your dog and cause him to have an infestation. Symptoms include hair loss and intense itching. The mite is very illusive and therefore difficult to diagnose through skin scraping. Topical treatment is often started based on clinical signs of the patient and his owners.

Common Health Concerns for the Lhasa

Lhasa Apsos are generally healthy by nature, but because Apso fanciers want to keep the breed healthy, they are trying to identify and address health issues specific to the Apso. If dogs are affected with characteristics that are not strengthening the breed, they are not used in breeding programs. Breeders are hoping to get close to a perfectly healthy Apso. The following is not an attempt to address every possible genetic defect seen in dogs, only those specific to Lhasa Apsos.

DRY EYE

Dry eye is a condition that causes the eye to dry out because the tear glands fail to produce a normal amount of tears. The condition, which is hereditary in

Squeeze eye ointment into the lower lid.

Lhasas, can vary in severity, but if left untreated will result in a complete shutdown of the tear producing cells. Symptoms include chronically infected eyes, squinting and pain. Application of artificial tears or lubricating ointments will ease the symptoms but must be performed several times a day. As long as there is some gland function, treatment with a special dilution of cyclosporine will stimulate tear production. Dosing every eight hours for severe cases or every two or three days for mild cases eases the burden of an intense medication schedule.

PROGRESSIVE RETINAL ATROPHY

Progressive Retinal Atrophy (PRA) is a genetic disease of the retina inherited by a simple recessive gene. The sad feature of PRA is that its onset does not occur until later in life. It is not detectable in puppies and affected relatives are the only indicator of the condition. Though the frequency of the disease in Lhasa Apsos is debatable, it does occur. Clinical signs in an adult dog include varying degrees of sight loss and dilated pupils. The disease is properly diagnosed by a board certified veterinary ophthalmologist who uses special instruments to view the retinal area. There is no cure.

RENAL DYSPLASIA

There are several documented types of renal or kidney disease but renal dysplasia is a hereditary defect seen only in Lhasa Apsos and Shih Tzus. The normal kidney is composed of thousands of tiny filtering devices called glomeruli that filter waste products out of the blood and excrete them as urine. In a dog with renal dysplasia, glomeruli fail to grow and develop with the rest of the puppy's body and eventually reach a critical point where the body is too large for the dwarfed kidney to effectively function. Sometimes the body will reach adult size only to have the weakened kidney deteriorate. The body develops renal poisoning which results in death. Unfortunately, renal failure is very painful due to the dog's massive thirst, nausea and excessive urination. A dog suffering from severe renal disease should be humanely euthanized.

PATELLAR LUXATION

Patellar luxation is a hereditary defect caused by a recessive gene. The condition is the result of a shallow patellar groove, the area of the knee where the patella (kneecap) slides, or the shortening of the ligament holding the patella in place. An additional complication may be the rotation of the tibia, the bone composing the lower half of the knee joint. These abnormalities cause the kneecap to pop in and out of the groove while the dog walks. Evidence of luxating patellas can be seen in a limp or "skipping" gait, a sign that the dog is trying to ease discomfort in the joint and slip the patella back in the groove. Additional signs include muscle wasting, failure to extend the rear leg while walking and a stance with rear legs under instead of behind the body. Usually dogs with luxating patellas are reluctant to jump and use stairs.

The lack of strength in the joint can lead to other problems such as ruptured meniscus, the fluid-filled sack in the joint, and a ruptured cruciate tendon, a stabilizing tendon inside the joint itself.

Patellar luxation in Lhasa Apsos is usually not debilitating because the breed is small and therefore does not bear too much pressure on the joint. It is best to keep an affected dog from gaining too much weight which would exacerbate the condition.

HIP DYSPLASIA

Hip dysplasia is a multigene genetic defect found in many large and giant breeds and some smaller dogs. The disease manifests itself in several ways. The normal hip joint is a ball and socket: The top of the femur or thigh bone is the ball, and the pelvis is the socket. In a dog with dysplasia, the ball is flattened and may be rough. The diseased socket, instead of cupping tightly around the ball, is also flat. This defective structure causes the bones to wear unevenly against each other, leading to lameness, arthritis and subsequent muscle wasting. Hip dysplasia is generally less debilitating in small dogs than larger dogs because there is less weight bearing down on the joints. However, an affected animal may still require pain medication and even surgery to ease discomfort.

The Orthopedic Foundation for Animals certifies patellar soundness and is a national registry for hip soundness. If you are concerned about patella and hip health, ask for the certification of your puppy's parents. This will not guarantee that your Apso is sound, but if both parents are unaffected, the incidence of dysplasia in their offspring will be low.

HYPOTHYROIDISM

Hypothyroidism is characterized by the thyroid gland's inability to produce adequate thyroid hormone for the body's needs. Symptoms include obesity, lethargy, thinning coat and a doughy abdomen. Affected animals instinctively seek out the warmest areas in the house, often laying by heat ducts for hours. Secondary yeast ear infections are also common. Diagnosis must be made through a blood test that evaluates four separate increments of thyroid function. Medication for the specific deficiency is then prescribed. Treatment should never be made without testing because it may not remedy the appropriate deficiency.

Hypothyroidism will often lead to other hormonal problems such as infertility, inability to have an estrus cycle in females, reduced sperm production in males, allergies, Cushings disease and secondary staph skin infections. Hypothyroidism has familial tendencies and often increases in severity with each generation.

ALLERGIES

Food allergies are discussed in chapter 5. Lhasa Apsos can also fall victim to inhalant allergies like dust mites, molds and fleas. The problem is not rampant in the breed, but does occur with enough frequency to be of concern. Allergies tend to be passed on genetically. Allergy symptoms in dogs show up in the skin and include a thinning coat, itching, thickened skin, weeping or infected skin. The ears are also frequently affected with secondary yeast infections.

Allergy symptoms can be controlled, but treatment is time-consuming and expensive. In severe cases, allergy testing is used to help identify the antagonist. Removal of the antagonist from the Apso's environment is then advised, but if this is not possible, the use of allergens

> ### WHEN TO CALL THE VET
>
> In any emergency situation, you should call your veterinarian immediately. You can make the difference in your dog's life by staying as calm as possible when you call and by giving the doctor or the assistant as much information as possible before you leave for the clinic. That way, the vet will be able to take immediate, specific action to remedy your dog's situation.
>
> Emergencies include acute abdominal pain, suspected poisoning, snakebite, burns, frostbite, shock, dehydration, abnormal vomiting or bleeding, and deep wounds. You are the best judge of your dog's health, as you live with and observe him every day. Don't hesitate to call your veterinarian if you suspect trouble.

or "allergy shots" is the next step. Allergy testing and allergy shots are procedures best overseen by a specialist. Use of corticosteroids to ease secondary symptoms should be limited because the long-term effects can be debilitating and life shortening.

If any of the conditions are of special concern to you as a potential Lhasa Apso owner, consult the breeder and ask to see the verification of any testing that has been done on the prospective Apso or his parents. Do remember, however, that no dog is perfect and that any Lhasa Apso you come in contact with will probably have some imperfection. Unless the condition is debilitating or life threatening, you need not pass over the Apso when you are selecting a pet. As long as the positive aspects of this Apso outweigh the negative, he will most likely make a suitable companion and will do well with proper care in a loving home.

SPAYING AND NEUTERING

Having dogs safely sterilized is a common practice among the pet owning community. In the female, the ovaries and uterus are surgically removed through an abdominal incision. In the male, the testicles are removed through a small incision through the skin layers just above the scrotum. Sterilization is an important part of taking good care of your Lhasa Apso's health. Spaying your female Apso reduces the chance of endometritis (inflammation of the uterine lining), pyometra (uterine infection) and unwanted pregnancies. Also, ovarian and mammary cancers are significantly reduced when the female is spayed. Studies have shown that the number of estrus cycles experienced by a female dog is directly proportional to the incidence of mammary cancer. Castrating your male eliminates the chance of prostrate and testicular problems, including cancer. If dogs are altered when they are young, males never exhibit sexual behavior, including urine marking.

It is not necessary for the male or female dog to experience mating to be "fulfilled" in life. Dogs operate on instinct—they do not feel "cheated" when they are not permitted to procreate nor do they miss the breeding or whelping process. A spayed female is never subjected to the complications of delivery (such as a cesarean section, mastitis or uterine infection). Mothers debilitated by surgery or disease cannot take care of their puppies, which forces the owner to raise the litter themselves. With some mothers, instinct simply fails and they reject their puppies. In such cases, the owner must take over the care and feeding of the puppies.

A male, if neutered at a young age, does not mark his territory on the sofa, "ride" the legs of small children or become aggressive with other dogs. He will simply be a loving companion.

Some people feel that their Apso's good health or excellent temperament are reasons to breed their pet. Breeding your Apso is not necessary for your pet or the Lhasa Apso community in general. There is no guarantee that any positive traits in the parents will be present in the puppies because genetic inheritance tends to be random. Understand that leaving your pet intact is gambling with his health. Do yourself and your Apso a good deed . . . remember that you obtained your Apso as a loving companion, so spay or neuter him or her.

ADVANTAGES OF SPAY/NEUTER

The greatest advantage of spaying (for females) or neutering (for males) your dog is that you are guaranteed your dog will not produce puppies. There are too many puppies already available for too few homes. There are other advantages as well.

ADVANTAGES OF SPAYING

No messy heats.

No "suitors" howling at your windows or waiting in your yard.

Decreased incidences of pyometra (disease of the uterus) and breast cancer.

ADVANTAGES OF NEUTERING

Lessens male aggressive and territorial behaviors, but doesn't affect the dog's personality. Behaviors are often owner-induced, so neutering is not the only answer, but it is a good start.

Prevents the need to roam in search of bitches in season.

Decreased incidences of urogenital diseases.

Household Dangers

Many items around the house can cause great harm, even death, to your Lhasa Apso. The following common household items that are dangerous to your Apso if ingested.

*Some of the
many household
substances harm-
ful to your dog.*

- Acetaminophen and ibuprofen are fine for humans but will cause acute liver shutdown in dogs. Treatment includes hospitalization on intravenous fluid therapy and stomach tubing with activated charcoal. *Never* treat your Apso with these medications.

- Aspirin can cause acute stomach bleeding and blood thinning in dogs; it should never be given to your Apso.

- Human prescription drugs, especially heart medication, blood pressure medication, antidepressants, allergy relievers and hormone replacement, require immediate consultation with your Lhasa's veterinarian. Symptoms and treatment vary with each drug.

- Mouse and rat poisons contain chemicals that prevent the blood from clotting. They show their effect about eight days after ingestion with symptoms of lethargy, skin bruising and uncontrolled bleeding into the chest or abdomen. Many brands contain flavors that are enticing to rodents and unfortunately, also to dogs. Vomiting must be induced immediately, followed by activated charcoal. After discharge from a veterinary hospital, further treatment includes vitamin K replacement and rechecking the dog's blood clotting time.

- Antifreeze tastes sweet and attracts animals, but one lick will be fatal if not treated *immediately*. Once symptoms of staggering and excessive thirst appear hours later, it is probably too late for effective treatment. Eventually, uncontrollable seizures and kidney failure lead to death. Treatment includes intravenous fluid therapy, activated charcoal and medications to stimulate kidney function.

- Salt, in excess, will cause sodium toxicity and will lead to acute seizures and death. Children's clays and salted sidewalks are common sources of excess salt.

- Fertilizers and pesticides do not seem to be very tasty, but dogs have been known to ingest them. The chemicals in each product varies. If your Apso has eaten or walked in any of these products it is best to contact your veterinarian for advice.

Ingesting Non-Food Items

Bones can cause intestinal upset or even blockage. Consult your veterinarian because, in some cases, inducing vomiting is recommended but if the bones are splintered, vomiting can cause injury to the stomach and esophagus.

Clothing, such as socks and undergarments, are sometimes eaten because they smell like the owner and seem like real treats. Such items will do harm if they become lodged in the stomach or intestinal tract. Sometimes this material will pass through the colon, but if symptoms of vomiting, abdominal pain, loss of appetite and small amounts of diarrhea appear, x-rays and probable surgical intervention may be necessary to save your Apso's life. Left untreated, foreign bodies can cause intestinal perforation and fatal peritonitis.

Consult your veterinarian immediately if you think your Lhasa Apso has ingested any drug or foreign object. Timing is important—your veterinarian may want you to induce vomiting at home. Because your Apso's stomach empties its contents in two to four hours, inducing vomiting after that time is ineffective. Be prepared to be as specific as possible in describing what you believe your Apso has ingested as well as the time it was swallowed. Labels will usually describe the ingredients of the product. If a veterinarian is not available, call your local poison control center for advice.

First Aid

Although books should never be used instead of the advice and care of your veterinarian, comprehensive books like the *Dog Owner's Home Veterinary Handbook* by Delbert G. Carlson, DVM and James M. Giffin, MD (Howell Book House) or *Puppy Owner's Veterinary Care*

Book by James DeBitetto, DVM (Howell Book House) can help you identify health problems and advise you in an emergency situation.

CHOKING

Because dogs will put almost anything in their mouths, they are likely candidates for choking (puppies are particularly predisposed to this problem). Most objects

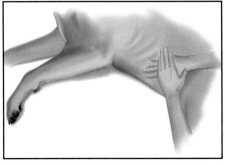

lodged in the throat will not occlude the air passage, but if your Apso looks like he is trying to vomit, he needs immediate veterinary attention. Do not stick your fingers down your Lhasa's throat while he is conscious—if he struggles you may inadvertently push the object further down or be bitten. If your Apso suddenly has trouble breathing, hold him upside down and shake or administer slaps to the back. You may try a chest compression to unblock the airway. If your Lhasa Apso is unconscious, try putting your fingers down his throat and feeling for a foreign object. Whether the object is extracted or not, an immediate trip to the veterinarian is required to check for injury or additional foreign objects.

Applying abdominal thrusts can save a choking dog.

HEMORRHAGE

If your Lhasa Apso is bleeding, try to keep yourself and the dog calm. Treatment varies depending on the location of the bleeding. Blood coming from the mouth or nose should receive immediate veterinary attention. Although your Apso is unlikely to bleed to death, the irritation from the blood will cause your Apso to sneeze and toss his head. This bleeding can be caused by a lost tooth, an abscess, an injury or in older dogs, a tumor.

Blood coming from a skin surface can be controlled by direct pressure with a clean rag or towel. A bleeding foot should be wrapped in a pressure bandage for the trip to your veterinarian.

If the bleeding has a pumping or spurting action, apply a thick bandage directly over the area for an immediate trip to your veterinarian. This is arterial bleeding and, if not fatal, will take a long time to clot.

Never put medicines, powders or water in an open wound. Applying these items can irritate, cause infection and/or dislodge a blood clot.

Use a scarf or old hose to make a temporary muzzle, as shown.

HEAT STROKE

Lhasa Apsos seem to be better equipped for cold rather than hot weather; therefore, special care should be taken to keep your Apso cool. The following is a list of precautions to take when the weather is sunny and warm:

1. Don't leave your Apso inside a closed car.

2. Don't keep him confined in a pen without shade.

3. Don't keep him any place where the temperature is approximately the same as your Apso's (above 95°F).

4. Don't allow him to exercise excessively.

5. Don't confine him anywhere that doesn't have ventilation.

6. Don't keep him anywhere that's very humid.

7. Don't leave him without fresh, cool water at any time.

Signs of heat stroke include rapid, shallow panting; a bright red tongue and gums; body temperature over 105°F; delirium and collapse. The best treatment is to bring the dog's high temperature down as quickly as possible. This can be done by wrapping your Apso (especially his head) in towels soaked in cold water, applying ice packs to the abdomen and offering cool (not cold or icy) water to drink. If your Apso vomits the water, do not give him anything to eat or drink.

Another method of cooling the dog down is to sponge his entire body with cool water or with a combination of cool water and alcohol. Transport your Apso to your veterinarian as soon as possible because heat stroke makes him susceptible to renal shutdown and other metabolic complications. Intravenous fluids and other medications are necessary to prevent permanent damage.

SPIDER BITES, INSECT BITES AND BEE STINGS

Because Lhasa Apsos are small, toxins from bee, wasp or hornet stings and spider or insect bites can cause a reaction as mild as a small welt to a reaction as severe as anaphylactic shock. This shock occurs most often if your Apso has been stung or bitten numerous times by more than one insect at the same time. Detection of an insect can be difficult in the Apso's thick hair. Nevertheless, when an insect is found biting or stinging your Apso or you find the result of a bite or sting on the skin, apply a cool compress. In cases of systemic welts, hives, reddened skin, red rash or swelling, a trip to your veterinarian is necessary for treatment. Swelling from either a sting or a spider or an insect bite is an allergic reaction and is evidenced by swollen lips, eyelids, muzzle and ears.

A FIRST-AID KIT

Keep a canine first-aid kit on hand for general care and emergencies. Check it periodically to make sure liquids haven't spilled or dried up, and replace medications and materials after they're used. Your kit should include:

Activated charcoal tablets

Adhesive tape
(1 and 2 inches wide)

Antibacterial ointment
(for skin and eyes)

Aspirin (buffered or enteric coated, *not* ibuprofen)

Bandages: Gauze rolls (1 and 2 inches wide) and dressing pads

Cotton balls

Diarrhea medicine

Dosing syringe

Hydrogen peroxide (3%)

Petroleum jelly

Rectal thermometer

Rubber gloves

Rubbing alcohol

Scissors

Tourniquet

Towel

Tweezers

These dogs are often nauseated and will vomit. If the swelling effects the throat area, causing shortness of breath, wheezing or collapse, immediate veterinary attention is imperative.

Periodically check your Apso's coat for harmful insects when he is outside.

SHOCK

Common causes of shock are dehydration due to prolonged vomiting and diarrhea, heat stroke, severe infections, burns, poisoning and hemorrhage. Traumas from fights with other animals, being hit by a car, extreme fright or allergic reactions can all cause your Lhasa Apso to go into shock.

Shock occurs when there is a lack of adequate blood flow to meet the needs of your Apso's body. The signs of shock are a drop in body temperature, shivering, listlessness, depression, weakness, cold feet and legs, pale skin and mucous membranes and a weak pulse. To help prevent further aggravation of shock, speak soothingly to your Apso and help him get comfortable. Cover your Apso with a towel or blanket without wrapping him

Run your hands regularly over your dog to feel for any injuries.

93

tightly. Transport him to your veterinarian as soon as possible.

Euthanasia

Typical old age diseases and conditions may appear in elderly dogs, and Lhasa Apsos are not exempt. Heart failure, diabetes, liver disease and more often, kidney failure are the common maladies seen in aged Apsos. Most conditions are manageable to a certain extent, but even the best veterinary treatment may not relieve a dog's suffering. Sometimes, when a disease becomes unmanageable or the dog's condition worsens despite medical intervention, a decision must be made whether or not to continue his life.

In this situation, ask yourself: "Is the quality of life what it should be for my dog?" The Lhasa Apso is a very dignified, independent breed and may feel humiliated or depressed by his inability to perform his normal functions (such as sounding alarm, watching over his family or sustaining his potty habits). An Apso incapacitated by disease or extreme old age is usually not happy unless excellent supportive care can be provided. In most cases just keeping him alive may not be the best decision for your Apso. It is unfortunate that aged dogs do not all pass away in their sleep; however, when life is no longer dignified and the dog's natural death will be preceded by great pain, euthanasia can be a blessed option. Consult your veterinarian regarding this decision.

Your Happy, Healthy Pet

Your Dog's Name _____

Name on Your Dog's Pedigree (if your dog has one) _____

_____

Where Your Dog Came From _____

_____

Your Dog's Birthday _____

Your Dog's Veterinarian

    Name _____

    Address _____

    Phone Number_____

    Emergency Number_____

Your Dog's Health

    Vaccines

    type _____ date given _____

    type _____ date given _____

    type _____ date given _____

    type _____ date given _____

    Heartworm

    date tested _____ type used_____ start date _____

Your Dog's License Number_____

Groomer's Name and Number _____

Dogsitter/Walker's Name and Number_____

Awards Your Dog Has Won

    Award _____ date earned _____

    Award _____ date earned _____

part three

Enjoying
your
Dog

chapter 8

Basic
Training

by Ian Dunbar, Ph.D., MRCVS

Training is the jewel in the crown—the most important aspect of doggy husbandry. There is no more important variable influencing dog behavior and temperament than the dog's education: A well-trained, well-behaved and good-natured puppydog is always a joy to live with, but an untrained and uncivilized dog can be a perpetual nightmare. Moreover, deny the dog an education and she will not have the opportunity to fulfill her own canine potential; neither will she have the ability to communicate effectively with her human companions.

Luckily, modern psychological training methods are easy, efficient, effective and, above all, considerably dog-friendly and user-friendly.

Doggy education is as simple as it is enjoyable. But before you can have a good time play-training with your new dog, you have to learn what to do and how to do it. There is no bigger variable influencing the success of dog training than the *owner's* experience and expertise. *Before you embark on the dog's education, you must first educate yourself.*

Basic Training for Owners

Ideally, basic owner training should begin well *before* you select your dog. Find out all you can about your chosen breed first, then master rudimentary training and handling skills. If you already have your puppydog, owner training is a dire emergency—the clock is ticking! Especially for puppies, the first few weeks at home are the most important and influential days in the dog's life. Indeed, the cause of most adolescent and adult problems may be traced back to the initial days the pup explores her new home. This is the time to establish the *status quo*—to teach the puppydog how you would like her to behave and so prevent otherwise quite predictable problems.

In addition to consulting breeders and breed books such as this one (which understandably have a positive breed bias), seek out as many pet owners with your breed as you can find. Good points are obvious. What you want to find out are the breed-specific *problems,* so you can nip them in the bud. In particular, you should talk to owners with *adolescent* dogs and make a list of all anticipated problems. Most important, *test drive* at least half a dozen adolescent and adult dogs of your breed yourself. An 8-week-old puppy is deceptively easy to handle, but she will acquire adult size, speed and strength in just four months, so you should learn now what to prepare for.

Puppy and pet dog training classes offer a convenient venue to locate pet owners and observe dogs in action. For a list of suitable trainers in your area, contact the Association of Pet Dog Trainers (see chapter 13). You may also begin your basic owner training by observing

other owners in class. Watch as many classes and test
drive as many dogs as possible. Select an upbeat, dog-
friendly, people-friendly, fun-and-games, puppydog pet
training class to learn the ropes. Also, watch training
videos and read training books. You must find out what
to do and how to do it *before* you have to do it.

Principles of Training

Most people think training comprises teaching the dog
to do things such as sit, speak and roll over, but even a
4-week-old pup knows how to do these things already.
Instead, the first step in training involves teaching
the dog human words for each dog behavior and activity and for each aspect of the dog's environment. That
way you, the owner, can more easily participate in the
dog's domestic education by directing her to perform
specific actions appropriately, that is, at the right time,
in the right place and so on. Training opens communication channels, enabling an educated dog to at least
understand her owner's requests.

In addition to teaching a dog *what* we want her to
do, it is also necessary to teach her *why* she should do
what we ask. Indeed, 95 percent of training revolves
around motivating the dog *to want to do* what we want.
Dogs often understand what their owners want; they
just don't see the point of doing it—especially when
the owner's repetitively boring and seemingly senseless
instructions are totally at odds with much more press-
ing and exciting doggy distractions. It is not so much
the dog that is being stubborn or dominant; rather, it
is the owner who has failed to acknowledge the dog's
needs and feelings and to approach training from the
dog's point of view.

THE MEANING OF INSTRUCTIONS

The secret to successful training is learning how to use
training lures to predict or prompt specific behaviors—
to coax the dog to do what you want *when* you want.
Any highly valued object (such as a treat or toy) may be
used as a lure, which the dog will follow with her eyes

and nose. Moving the lure in specific ways entices the dog to move her nose, head and entire body in specific ways. In fact, by learning the art of manipulating various lures, it is possible to teach the dog to assume virtually any body position and perform any action. Once you have control over the expression of the dog's behaviors and can elicit any body position or behavior at will, you can easily teach the dog to perform on request.

Teach your dog words for each activity she needs to know, like down.

Tell your dog what you want her to do, use a lure to entice her to respond correctly, then profusely praise and maybe reward her once she performs the desired action. For example, verbally request "Tina, sit!" while you move a squeaky toy upwards and backwards over the dog's muzzle (lure-movement and hand signal), smile knowingly as she looks up (to follow the lure) and sits down (as a result of canine anatomical engineering), then praise her to distraction ("Gooood Tina!"). Squeak the toy, offer a training treat and give your dog and yourself a pat on the back.

Being able to elicit desired responses over and over enables the owner to reward the dog over and over. Consequently, the dog begins to think training is fun. For example, the more the dog is rewarded for sitting, the more she enjoys sitting. Eventually the dog comes to realize that, whereas most sitting is appreciated, sitting immediately upon request usually prompts especially enthusiastic praise and a slew of high-level rewards. The dog begins to sit on cue much of the time, showing that she is starting to grasp the meaning of the owner's verbal request and hand signal.

WHY COMPLY?

Most dogs enjoy initial lure-reward training and are only too happy to comply with their owners' wishes. Unfortunately, repetitive drilling without appreciative feedback tends to diminish the dog's enthusiasm until she eventually fails to see the point of complying anymore. Moreover, as the dog approaches adolescence she becomes more easily distracted as she develops other interests. Lengthy sessions with repetitive exercises tend to bore and demotivate both parties. If it's not fun, the owner doesn't do it and neither does the dog.

Integrate training into your dog's life: The greater number of training sessions each day and the *shorter* they are, the more willingly compliant your dog will

become. Make sure to have a short (just a few seconds) training interlude before every enjoyable canine activity. For example, ask your dog to sit to greet people, to sit before you throw her Frisbee and to sit for her supper. Really, sitting is no different from a canine "Please."

To train your dog, you need gentle hands, a loving heart and a good attitude.

Also, include numerous short training interludes during every enjoyable canine pastime, for example, when playing with the dog or when she is running in the park. In this fashion, doggy distractions may be effectively converted into rewards for training. Just as all games have rules, fun becomes training . . . and training becomes fun.

Eventually, rewards actually become unnecessary to continue motivating your dog. If trained with consideration and kindness, performing the desired behaviors will become self-rewarding and, in a sense, your dog will motivate herself. Just as it is not necessary to reward a human companion during an enjoyable walk in the park, or following a game of tennis, it is hardly necessary to reward our best friend—the dog— for walking by our side or while playing fetch. Human company during enjoyable activities is reward enough for most dogs.

Even though your dog has become self-motivating, it's still good to praise and pet her a lot and offer rewards once in a while, especially for a good job well done. And if for no other reason, praising and rewarding others is good for the human heart.

Punishment

Without a doubt, lure-reward training is by far the best way to teach: Entice your dog to do what you want and then reward her for doing so. Unfortunately, a human shortcoming is to take the good for granted and to moan and groan at the bad. Specifically, the dog's many good behaviors are ignored while the owner focuses on punishing the dog for making mistakes. In extreme cases, instruction is *limited* to punishing mistakes made by a trainee dog, child, employee or husband, even though it has been proven punishment training is notoriously inefficient and ineffective and is decidedly unfriendly and combative. It teaches the dog that training is a drag, almost as quickly as it teaches the dog to dislike her trainer. Why treat our best friends like our worst enemies?

Punishment training is also much more laborious and time consuming. Whereas it takes only a finite amount of time to teach a dog what to chew, for example, it takes much, much longer to punish the dog for each and every mistake. Remember, *there is only one right way!* So why not teach that right way from the outset?!

To make matters worse, punishment training causes severe lapses in the dog's reliability. Since it is obviously impossible to punish the dog each and every time she misbehaves, the dog quickly learns to distinguish between those times when she must comply (so as to avoid impending punishment) and those times when she need not comply, because punishment is impossible. Such times include when the dog is off leash and 6 feet away, when the owner is otherwise engaged (talking to a friend, watching television, taking a shower, tending to the baby or chatting on the telephone) or when the dog is left at home alone.

Instances of misbehavior will be numerous when the owner is away, because even when the dog complied in the owner's looming presence, she did so unwillingly. The dog was forced to act against her will, rather than molding her will to want to please. Hence, when the owner is absent, not only does the dog know she need not comply, she simply does not want to. Again, the trainee is not a stubborn vindictive beast, but rather the trainer has failed to teach. Punishment training invariably creates unpredictable Jekyll and Hyde behavior.

Trainer's Tools

Many training books extol the virtues of a vast array of training paraphernalia and electronic and metallic gizmos, most of which are designed for canine restraint, correction and punishment, rather than for actual facilitation of doggy education. In reality, most effective training tools are not found in stores; they come from within ourselves. In addition to a willing dog, all you really need is a functional human brain, gentle hands, a loving heart and a good attitude.

In terms of equipment, all dogs do require a quality buckle collar to sport dog tags and to attach the leash (for safety and to comply with local leash laws). Hollow chew toys (like Kongs or sterilized longbones) and a dog bed or collapsible crate are musts for housetraining. Three additional tools are required:

1. specific lures (training treats and toys) to predict and prompt specific desired behaviors;

2. rewards (praise, affection, training treats and toys) to reinforce for the dog what a lot of fun it all is; and

3. knowledge—how to convert the dog's favorite activities and games (potential distractions to training) into "life-rewards," which may be employed to facilitate training.

The most powerful of these is *knowledge*. Education is the key! Watch training classes, participate in training classes, watch videos, read books, enjoy play-training with your dog and then your dog will say "Please," and your dog will say "Thank you!"

Housetraining

If dogs were left to their own devices, certainly they would chew, dig and bark for entertainment and then no doubt highlight a few areas of their living space with sprinkles of urine, in much the same way we decorate by hanging pictures. Consequently, when we ask a dog to live with us, we must teach her *where* she may dig, *where* she may perform her toilet duties, *what* she may chew and *when* she may bark. After all, when left at home alone for many hours, we cannot expect the dog to amuse herself by completing crosswords or watching the soaps on TV!

Also, it would be decidedly unfair to keep the house rules a secret from the dog, and then get angry and punish the poor critter for inevitably transgressing rules she did not even know existed. Remember: Without adequate education and guidance, the dog will be forced to establish her own rules—doggy rules—and most probably will be at odds with the owner's view of domestic living.

Since most problems develop during the first few days the dog is at home, prospective dog owners must be certain they are quite clear about the principles of housetraining *before* they get a dog. Early misbehaviors quickly become established as the *status quo*—

becoming firmly entrenched as hard-to-break bad habits, which set the precedent for years to come. Make sure to teach your dog good habits right from the start. Good habits are just as hard to break as bad ones!

Ideally, when a new dog comes home, try to arrange for someone to be present as much as possible during the first few days (for adult dogs) or weeks for puppies. With only a little forethought, it is surprisingly easy to find a puppy sitter, such as a retired person, who would be willing to eat from your refrigerator and watch your television while keeping an eye on the newcomer to encourage the dog to play with chew toys and to ensure she goes outside on a regular basis.

POTTY TRAINING

To teach the dog where to relieve herself:

1. never let her make a single mistake;
2. let her know where you want her to go; and
3. handsomely reward her for doing so: "GOOOOOOOD DOG!!!" liver treat, liver treat, liver treat!

Preventing Mistakes

A single mistake is a training disaster, since it heralds many more in future weeks. And each time the dog soils the house, this further reinforces the dog's unfortunate preference for an indoor, carpeted toilet. *Do not let an unhousetrained dog have full run of the house.*

When you are away from home, or cannot pay full attention, confine the dog to an area where elimination is appropriate, such as an outdoor run or, better still, a small, comfortable indoor kennel with access to an outdoor run. When confined in this manner, most dogs will naturally housetrain themselves.

If that's not possible, confine the dog to an area, such as a utility room, kitchen, basement or garage, where elimination may not be desired in the long run but as an interim measure it is certainly preferable to doing it all around the house. Use newspaper to cover the floor of the dog's day room. The newspaper may be used to soak up the urine and to wrap up and dispose of the feces. Once your dog develops a preferred spot for eliminating, it is only necessary to cover that part of the floor with newspaper. The smaller papered area may then be moved (only a little each day) towards the door to the outside. Thus the dog will develop the tendency to go to the door when she needs to relieve herself.

Never confine an unhousetrained dog to a crate for long periods. Doing so would force the dog to soil the crate and ruin its usefulness as an aid for housetraining (see the following discussion).

Teaching Where

In order to teach your dog where you would like her to do her business, you have to be there to direct the proceedings—an obvious, yet often neglected, fact of life. In order to be there to teach the dog *where* to go, you need to know *when* she needs to go. Indeed, the success of housetraining depends on the owner's ability to predict these times. Certainly, a regular feeding schedule will facilitate prediction somewhat, but there is nothing like "loading the deck" and influencing the timing of the outcome yourself!

The first few weeks at home are the most important and influential in your dog's life.

Whenever you are at home, make sure the dog is under constant supervision and/or confined to a small area. If already well trained, simply instruct the dog to lie down in her bed or basket. Alternatively, confine the dog to a crate (doggy den) or tie-down (a short, 18-inch lead that can be clipped to an eye hook in the baseboard near her bed). Short-term close confinement strongly inhibits urination and defecation, since the dog does not want to soil her sleeping area. Thus, when you release the puppydog each hour, she will definitely need to urinate immediately and defecate every third or fourth hour. Keep the dog confined to her doggy den and take her to her intended toilet area each hour, every hour and on the hour.

When taking your dog outside, instruct her to sit quietly before opening the door—she will soon learn to sit by the door when she needs to go out!

Teaching Why

Being able to predict when the dog needs to go enables the owner to be on the spot to praise and reward the dog. Each hour, hurry the dog to the intended toilet area in the yard, issue the appropriate instruction ("Go pee!" or "Go poop!"), then give the dog three to four minutes to produce. Praise and offer a couple of training treats when successful. The treats are important because many people fail to praise their dogs with feeling . . . and housetraining is hardly the time for understatement. So either loosen up and enthusiastically praise that dog: "Wuzzzer-wuzzer-wuzzer, hoooser good wuffer den? Hoooo went pee for Daddy?" Or say "Good dog!" as best you can and offer the treats for effect.

Following elimination is an ideal time for a spot of play-training in the yard or house. Also, an empty dog may be allowed greater freedom around the house for the next half hour or so, just as long as you keep an eye out to make sure she does not get into other kinds of mischief. If you are preoccupied and cannot pay full attention, confine the dog to her doggy den once more to enjoy a peaceful snooze or to play with her many chew toys.

If your dog does not eliminate within the allotted time outside—no biggie! Back to her doggy den, and then try again after another hour.

As I own large dogs, I always feel more relaxed walking an empty dog, knowing that I will not need to finish our stroll weighted down with bags of feces!

Beware of falling into the trap of walking the dog to get her to eliminate. The good ol' dog walk is such an enormous highlight in the dog's life that it represents the single biggest potential reward in domestic dogdom. However, when in a hurry, or during inclement weather, many owners abruptly terminate the walk the moment the dog has done her business. This, in effect, severely punishes the dog for doing the right thing, in the right place at the right time. Consequently, many dogs become strongly inhibited from eliminating outdoors because they know it will signal an abrupt end to an otherwise thoroughly enjoyable walk.

Instead, instruct the dog to relieve herself in the yard prior to going for a walk. If you follow the above instructions, most dogs soon learn to eliminate on cue. As soon as the dog eliminates, praise (and offer a treat or two)—"Good dog! Let's go walkies!" Use the walk as a reward for eliminating in the yard. If the dog does not go, put her back in her doggy den and think about a walk later on. You will find with a "No feces—no walk" policy, your dog will become one of the fastest defecators in the business.

If you do not have a backyard, instruct the dog to eliminate right outside your front door prior to the walk. Not only will this facilitate clean up and disposal of the feces in your own trash can but, also, the walk may again be used as a colossal reward.

CHEWING AND BARKING

Short-term close confinement also teaches the dog that occasional quiet moments are a reality of domestic living. Your puppydog is extremely impressionable during her first few weeks at home. Regular confinement at this time soon exerts a calming influence over the dog's personality. Remember, once the dog is housetrained and calmer, there will be a whole lifetime ahead for the dog to enjoy full run of the house and garden. On the other hand, by letting the newcomer have unrestricted access to the entire household and allowing her to run willy-nilly, she will most certainly develop a bunch of behavior problems in short order, no doubt necessitating confinement later in life. It would not be fair to remedially restrain and confine a dog you have trained, through neglect, to run free.

When confining the dog, make sure she always has an impressive array of suitable chew toys. Kongs and sterilized longbones (both readily available from pet stores) make the best chew toys, since they are hollow and may be stuffed with treats to heighten the dog's interest. For example, by stuffing the little hole at the top of a Kong with a small piece of freeze-dried liver, the dog will not want to leave it alone.

Remember, treats do not have to be junk food and they certainly should not represent extra calories. Rather, treats should be part of each dog's regular daily diet: Some food may be served in the dog's bowl for breakfast and dinner, some food may be used as training treats, and some food may be used for stuffing chew toys. I regularly stuff my dogs' many Kongs with different shaped biscuits and kibble.

Make sure your puppy has suitable chew toys.

The kibble seems to fall out fairly easily, as do the oval-shaped biscuits, thus rewarding the dog instantaneously for checking out the chew toys. The bone-shaped biscuits fall out after a while, rewarding the dog for worrying at the chew toy. But the triangular biscuits never come out. They remain inside the Kong as lures, maintaining the dog's fascination with her chew toy. To further focus the dog's interest, I always make sure to flavor the triangular biscuits by rubbing them with a little cheese or freeze-dried liver.

To teach come, call your dog, open your arms as a welcoming signal, wave a toy or a treat and praise for every step in your direction.

If stuffed chew toys are reserved especially for times the dog is confined, the puppydog will soon learn to enjoy quiet moments in her doggy den and she will quickly develop a chew-toy habit— a good habit! This is a simple *autoshaping* process; all the owner has to do is set up the situation and the dog all but trains herself— easy and effective. Even when the dog is given run of the house, her first inclination will be to indulge her rewarding chew-toy habit rather than destroy less-attractive household articles, such as curtains, carpets, chairs and compact disks. Similarly, a chew-toy chewer will be less inclined to scratch and chew herself excessively. Also, if the dog busies herself as a recreational chewer, she will be less inclined to develop into a recreational barker or digger when left at home alone.

Stuff a number of chew toys whenever the dog is left confined and remove the extra-special-tasting treats when you return. Your dog will now amuse herself with her chew toys before falling asleep and then resume playing with her chew toys when she expects you to return. Since most owner-absent misbehavior happens right after you leave and right before your expected return, your puppydog will now be conveniently preoccupied with her chew toys at these times.

Come and Sit

Most puppies will happily approach virtually anyone, whether called or not; that is, until they collide with adolescence and

develop other more important doggy interests, such as sniffing a multiplicity of exquisite odors on the grass. Your mission, Mr./Ms. Owner, is to teach and reward the pup for coming reliably, willingly and happily when called—and you have just three months to get it done. Unless adequately reinforced, your puppy's tendency to approach people will self-destruct by adolescence.

Call your dog ("Tina, come!"), open your arms (and maybe squat down) as a welcoming signal, waggle a treat or toy as a lure and reward the puppydog when she comes running. Do not wait to praise the dog until she reaches you—she may come 95 percent of the way and then run off after some distraction. Instead, praise the dog's *first* step towards you and continue praising enthusiastically for *every* step she takes in your direction.

When the rapidly approaching puppy dog is three lengths away from impact, instruct her to sit ("Tina, sit!") and hold the lure in front of you in an outstretched hand to prevent her from hitting you midchest and knocking you flat on your back! As Tina decelerates to nose the lure, move the treat upwards and backwards just over her muzzle with an upwards motion of your extended arm (palm-upwards). As the dog looks up to follow the lure, she will sit down (if she jumps up, you are holding the lure too high). Praise the dog for sitting. Move backwards and call her again. Repeat this many times over, always praising when Tina comes and sits; on occasion, reward her.

For the first couple of trials, use a training treat both as a lure to entice the dog to come and sit and as a reward for doing so. Thereafter, try to use different items as lures and rewards. For example, lure the dog with a Kong or Frisbee but reward her with a food treat. Or lure the dog with a food treat but pat her and throw a tennis ball as a reward. After just a few repetitions, dispense with the lures and rewards; the dog will begin to respond willingly to your verbal requests and hand signals just for the prospect of praise from your heart and affection from your hands.

Instruct every family member, friend and visitor how to get the dog to come and sit. Invite people over for a series of pooch parties; do not keep the pup a secret— let other people enjoy this puppy, and let the pup enjoy other people. Puppydog parties are not only fun, they easily attract a lot of people to help *you* train *your* dog. Unless you teach your dog how to meet people, that is, to sit for greetings, no doubt the dog will resort to jumping up. Then you and the visitors will get annoyed, and the dog will be punished. This is not fair. *Send out those invitations for puppy parties and teach your dog to be mannerly and socially acceptable.*

Even though your dog quickly masters obedient recalls in the house, her reliability may falter when playing in the backyard or local park. Ironically, it is *the owner* who has unintentionally trained the dog *not* to respond in these instances. By allowing the dog to play and run around and otherwise have a good time, but then to call the dog to put her on leash to take her home, the dog quickly learns playing is fun but training is a drag. Thus, playing in the park becomes a severe distraction, which works against training. Bad news!

Instead, whether playing with the dog off leash or on leash, request her to come at frequent intervals—say, every minute or so. On most occasions, praise and pet the dog for a few seconds while she is sitting, then tell her to go play again. For especially fast recalls, offer a couple of training treats and take the time to praise and pet the dog enthusiastically before releasing her. The dog will learn that coming when called is not necessarily the end of the play session, and neither is it the end of the world; rather, it signals an enjoyable, quality time-out with the owner before resuming play once more. In fact, playing in the park now becomes a very effective life-reward, which works to facilitate training by reinforcing each obedient and timely recall. Good news!

Sit, Down, Stand and Rollover

Teaching the dog a variety of body positions is easy for owner and dog, impressive for spectators and extremely useful for all. Using lure-reward techniques, it is possible to train several positions at once to verbal commands or hand signals (which impress the socks off onlookers).

Sit and **down**—the two control commands—prevent or resolve nearly a hundred behavior problems. For example, if the dog happily and obediently sits or lies down when requested, she cannot jump on visitors, dash out the front door, run around and chase her tail, pester other dogs, harass cats or annoy family, friends or strangers. Additionally, "Sit" or "Down" are the best emergency commands for off-leash control.

It is easier to teach and maintain a reliable sit than maintain a reliable recall. *Sit* is the purest and simplest of commands—either the dog is sitting or she is not. If there is any change of circumstances or potential danger in the park, for example, simply instruct the dog to sit. If she sits, you have a number of options: Allow the dog to resume playing when she is safe, walk up and put the dog on leash or call the dog. The dog will be much more likely to come when called if she has already acknowledged her compliance by sitting. If the dog does not sit in the park—train her to!

Stand and **rollover-stay** are the two positions for examining the dog. Your veterinarian will love you to distraction if you take a little time to teach the dog to stand still and roll over and play possum. Also, your vet bills will be smaller because it will take the veterinarian less time to examine your dog. The rollover-stay is an especially useful command and is really just a variation of the down-stay: Whereas the dog lies prone in the traditional down, she lies supine in the rollover-stay.

As with teaching come and sit, the training techniques to teach the dog to assume all other body positions on cue are user-friendly and dog-friendly. Simply give the appropriate request, lure the dog into the desired body position using a training treat or toy and then *praise* (and maybe reward) the dog as soon as she complies. Try not to touch the dog to get her to respond. If you teach the dog by guiding her into position, the dog will quickly learn that rump-pressure means sit, for example, but as yet you still have no control over your dog if she is just 6 feet away. It will still be necessary to teach the dog to sit on request. So do not make training a time-consuming two-step process; instead, teach the dog to sit to a verbal request or hand signal from the outset. Once the dog sits willingly when requested, by all means use your hands to pet the dog when she does so.

To teach **down** when the dog is already sitting, say "Tina, down!," hold the lure in one hand (palm down) and lower that hand to the floor between the dog's forepaws. As the dog lowers her head to follow the lure, slowly move the lure away from the dog just a fraction (in front of her paws). The dog will lie down as she stretches her nose forward to follow the lure. Praise the dog when she does so. If the dog stands up, you pulled the lure away too far and too quickly.

When teaching the dog to lie down from the standing position, say "Down" and lower the lure to the floor as before. Once the dog has lowered her forequarters and assumed a play bow, gently and slowly move the lure *towards* the dog between her forelegs. Praise the dog as soon as her rear end plops down.

After just a couple of trials it will be possible to alternate sits and downs and have the dog energetically perform doggy push-ups. Praise the dog a lot, and after half a dozen or so push-ups reward the dog with a training treat or toy. You will notice the more energetically you move your arm—upwards (palm up) to get the dog to sit, and downwards (palm down) to get the dog to lie down—the more energetically the dog responds to your requests. Now try training the dog in silence and you will notice she has also learned to respond to hand signals. Yeah! Not too shabby for the first session.

To teach **stand** from the sitting position, say "Tina, stand," slowly move the lure half a dog-length away from the dog's nose, keeping it at nose level, and praise the dog as she stands to follow the lure. As soon

Using a food lure to teach sit, down and stand. 1) "Phoenix, sit." 2) Hand palm upwards, move lure up and back over dog's muzzle. 3) "Good sit, Phoenix!" 4) "Phoenix, down." 5) Hand palm down-wards, move lure down to lie between dog's forepaws. 6) "Phoenix, off. Good down, Phoenix!" 7) "Phoenix, sit!" 8) Palm upwards, move lure up and back, keeping it close to dog's muzzle. 9) "Good sit, Phoenix!"

10) "Phoenix, stand!" 11) Move lure away from dog at nose height, then lower it a tad. 12) "Phoenix, off! Good stand, Phoenix!" 13) "Phoenix, down!" 14) Hand palm downwards, move lure down to lie between dog's forepaws. 15) "Phoenix, off! Good down-stay, Phoenix!" 16) "Phoenix, stand!" 17) Move lure away from dog's muzzle up to nose height. 18) "Phoenix, off! Good stand-stay, Phoenix. Now we'll make the vet and groomer happy!"

as the dog stands, lower the lure to just beneath the dog's chin to entice her to look down; otherwise she will stand and then sit immediately. To prompt the dog to stand from the down position, move the lure half a dog-length upwards and away from the dog, holding the lure at standing nose height from the floor.

Teaching **rollover** is best started from the down position, with the dog lying on one side, or at least with both hind legs stretched out on the same side. Say "Tina, bang!" and move the lure backwards and alongside the dog's muzzle to her elbow (on the side of her outstretched hind legs). Once the dog looks to the side and backwards, very slowly move the lure upwards to the dog's shoulder and backbone. Tickling the dog in the goolies (groin area) often invokes a reflex-raising of the hind leg as an appeasement gesture, which facilitates the tendency to roll over. If you move the lure too quickly and the dog jumps into the standing position, have patience and start again. As soon as the dog rolls onto her back, keep the lure stationary and mesmerize the dog with a relaxing tummy rub.

To teach **rollover-stay** when the dog is standing or moving, say "Tina, bang!" and give the appropriate hand signal (with index finger pointed and thumb cocked in true Sam Spade fashion), then in one fluid movement lure her to first lie down and then rollover-stay as above.

Teaching the dog to **stay** in each of the above four positions becomes a piece of cake after first teaching the dog not to worry at the toy or treat training lure. This is best accomplished by hand feeding dinner kibble. Hold a piece of kibble firmly in your hand and softly instruct "Off!" Ignore any licking and slobbering *for however long the dog worries at the treat*, but say "Take it!" and offer the kibble *the instant* the dog breaks contact with her muzzle. Repeat this a few times, and then up the ante and insist the dog remove her muzzle for one whole second before offering the kibble. Then progressively refine your criteria and have the dog not touch your hand (or treat) for longer and longer periods on each trial, such as for two seconds, four seconds, then six, ten, fifteen, twenty, thirty seconds and so on.

The dog soon learns: (1) worrying at the treat never gets results, whereas (2) noncontact is often rewarded after a variable time lapse.

Teaching *"Off!"* has many useful applications in its own right. Additionally, instructing the dog not to touch a training lure often produces spontaneous and magical stays. Request the dog to stand-stay, for example, and not to touch the lure. At first set your sights on a short two-second stay before rewarding the dog. (Remember, every long journey begins with a single step.) However, on subsequent trials, gradually and progressively increase the length of stay required to receive a reward. In no time at all your dog will stand calmly for a minute or so.

Relevancy Training

Once you have taught the dog what you expect her to do when requested to come, sit, lie down, stand, roll-over and stay, the time is right to teach the dog *why* she should comply with your wishes. The secret is to have many (*many*) extremely short training interludes (two to five seconds each) at numerous (*numerous*) times during the course of the dog's day. Especially work with the dog immediately *before* the dog's good times and *during* the dog's good times. For example, ask your dog to sit and/or lie down each time before opening doors, serving meals, offering treats and tummy rubs; ask the dog to perform a few controlled doggy push-ups before letting her off leash or throwing a tennis ball; and perhaps request the dog to sit-down-sit-stand-down-stand-rollover before inviting her to cuddle on the couch.

Similarly, request the dog to sit many times during play or on walks, and in no time at all the dog will be only too pleased to follow your instructions because she has learned that a compliant response heralds all sorts of goodies. Basically all you are trying to teach the dog is how to say please: "Please throw the tennis ball. Please may I snuggle on the couch."

Remember, it is important to keep training interludes short and to have many short sessions each and every day. The shortest (and most useful) session comprises asking the dog to sit and then go play during a play session. When trained this way, your dog will soon associate training with good times. In fact, the dog may be unable to distinguish between training and good times and, indeed, there should be no distinction. The warped concept that training involves forcing the dog to comply and/or dominating her will is totally at odds with the picture of a truly well-trained dog. In reality, enjoying a game of training with a dog is no different from enjoying a game of backgammon or tennis with a friend; and walking with a dog should be no different from strolling with a spouse, or with buddies on the golf course.

Walk by Your Side

Many people attempt to teach a dog to heel by putting her on a leash and physically correcting the dog when she makes mistakes. There are a number of things seriously wrong with this approach, the first being that most people do not want precision heeling; rather, they simply want the dog to follow or walk by their side. Second, when physically restrained during "training," even though the dog may grudgingly mope by your side when "handcuffed" on leash, let's see what happens when she is off leash. History! The dog is in the next county because she never enjoyed walking with you on leash and you have no control over her off leash. So let's just teach the dog off leash from the outset to *want* to walk with us. Third, if the dog has not been trained to heel, it is a trifle hasty to think about punishing the poor dog for making mistakes and breaking heeling rules she didn't even know existed. This is simply not fair! Surely, if the dog had been adequately taught how to heel, she would seldom make mistakes and hence there would be no need to correct the dog. Remember, each mistake and each correction (punishment) advertise the trainer's inadequacy, not the dog's. The dog is not stubborn, she is not stupid and she is not bad. Even if she were, she would still require training, so let's train her properly.

Let's teach the dog to *enjoy* following us and to *want* to walk by our side off leash. Then it will be easier to teach high-precision off-leash heeling patterns if desired. Before going on outdoor walks, it is necessary to teach the dog not to pull. Then it becomes easy to teach on-leash walking and heeling because the dog already wants to walk with you, she is familiar with the desired walking and heeling positions and she knows not to pull.

FOLLOWING

Start by training your dog to follow you. Many puppies will follow if you simply walk away from them and maybe click your fingers or chuckle. Adult dogs may require additional enticement to stimulate them to follow, such as a training lure or, at the very least, a lively trainer. To teach the dog to follow: (1) keep walking and (2) walk away from the dog. If the dog attempts to lead or lag, change pace; slow down if the dog forges too far ahead, but speed up if she lags too far behind. Say "Steady!" or "Easy!" each time before you slow down and "Quickly!" or "Hustle!" each time before you speed up, and the dog will learn to change pace on cue. If the dog lags or leads too far, or if she wanders right or left, simply walk quickly in the opposite direction and maybe even run away from the dog and hide.

Practicing is a lot of fun; you can set up a course in your home, yard or park to do this. Indoors, entice the dog to follow upstairs, into a bedroom, into the bathroom, downstairs, around the living room couch, zigzagging between dining room chairs and into the kitchen for dinner. Outdoors, get the dog to follow around park benches, trees, shrubs and along walkways and lines in the grass. (For safety outdoors, it is advisable to attach a long line on the dog, but never exert corrective tension on the line.)

Remember, following has a lot to do with attitude—*your* attitude! Most probably your dog will *not* want to follow Mr. Grumpy Troll with the personality of wilted lettuce. Lighten up—walk with a jaunty step, whistle a happy tune, sing, skip and tell jokes to your dog and she will be right there by your side.

BY YOUR SIDE

It is smart to train the dog to walk close on one side or the other—either side will do, your choice. When walking, jogging or cycling, it is generally bad news to have the dog suddenly cut in front of you. In fact, I train my dogs to walk "By my side" and "Other side"—both very useful instructions. It is possible to position the dog fairly accurately by looking to the appropriate side and clicking your fingers or slapping your thigh on that side. A precise positioning may be attained by holding a training lure, such as a chew toy, tennis ball or food treat. Stop and stand still several times throughout the walk, just as you would when window shopping or meeting a friend. Use the lure to make sure the dog slows down and stays close whenever you stop.

When teaching the dog to heel, we generally want her to sit in heel position when we stop. Teach heel

Using a toy to teach sit-heel-sit sequences: 1) "Phoenix, sit!" Standing still, move lure up and back over dog's muzzle . . . 2) to position dog sitting in heel position on your left side. 3) Say "Phoenix, heel!" and walk ahead, wagging lure in left hand. Change lure to right hand in preparation for sit signal. Say "Sit" and then . . .

position at the standstill and the dog will learn that the default heel position is sitting by your side (left or right—your choice, unless you wish to compete in obedience trials, in which case the dog must heel on the left).

Several times a day, stand up and call your dog to come and sit in heel position—"Tina, heel!" For example, instruct the dog to come to heel each time there are commercials on TV, or each time you turn a page of a novel, and the dog will get it in a single evening.

Practice straight-line heeling and turns separately. With the dog sitting at heel, teach her to turn in place. After each quarter-turn, half-turn or full turn in place, lure the dog to sit at heel. Now it's time for short straight-line heeling sequences, no more than a few steps at a time. Always think of heeling in terms of sit-heel-sit sequences—start and end with the dog in position and do your best to keep her there when moving. Progressively increase the number of steps in each sequence. When the dog remains close for 20 yards of straight-line heeling, it is time to add a few turns and then sign up for a happy-heeling obedience class to get some advice from the experts.

4) use hand signal to lure dog to sit as you stop. Eventually, dog will sit automatically at heel whenever you stop. 5) "Good dog!"

No Pulling on Leash

You can start teaching your dog not to pull on leash anywhere—in front of the television or outdoors—but regardless of location, you must not take a single step with tension in the leash. For a reason known only to dogs, even just a couple of paces of pulling on leash is intrinsically motivating and diabolically rewarding. Instead, attach the leash to the dog's collar, grasp the other end firmly with both hands held close to your chest, and stand still—do not budge an inch. Have somebody watch you with a stopwatch to time your progress, or else you will never believe this will work and so you will not even try the exercise, and your shoulder and the dog's neck will be traumatized for years to come.

Stand still and wait for the dog to stop pulling, and to sit and/or lie down. All dogs stop pulling and sit eventually. Most take only a couple of minutes; the all-time record is 22½ minutes. Time how long it takes. Gently praise the dog when she stops pulling, and as soon as she sits, enthusiastically praise the dog and take just one step forward, then immediately stand still. This single step usually demonstrates the ballistic reinforcing nature of pulling on leash; most dogs explode to the end of the leash, so be prepared for the strain. Stand firm and wait for the dog to sit again. Repeat this half a dozen times and you will probably notice a progressive reduction in the force of the dog's one-step explosions and a radical reduction in the time it takes for the dog to sit each time.

As the dog learns "Sit we go" and "Pull we stop," she will begin to walk forward calmly with each single step and automatically sit when you stop. Now try two steps before you stop. Wooooooo! Scary! When the dog has mastered two steps at a time, try for three. After each success, progressively increase the number of steps in the sequence: try four steps and then six, eight, ten and twenty steps before stopping. Congratulations! You are now walking the dog on leash.

Whenever walking with the dog (off leash or on leash), make sure you stop periodically to practice a few position commands and stays before instructing the dog to "Walk on!" (Remember, you want the dog to be compliant everywhere, not just in the kitchen when her dinner is at hand.) For example, stopping every 25 yards to briefly train the dog amounts to over 200 training interludes within a single 3-mile stroll. And each training session is in a different location. You will not believe the improvement within just the first mile of the first walk.

To put it another way, integrating training into a walk offers 200 separate opportunities to use the continuance of the walk as a reward to reinforce the dog's education. Moreover, some training interludes may comprise continuing education for the dog's walking skills: Alternate short periods of the dog walking calmly by your side with periods when the dog is allowed to sniff and investigate the environment. Now sniffing odors on the grass and meeting other dogs become rewards which reinforce the dog's calm and mannerly demeanor. Good Lord! Whatever next? Many enjoyable walks together of course. Happy trails!

THE IMPORTANCE OF TRICKS

Nothing will improve a dog's quality of life better than having a few tricks under her belt. Teaching any trick expands the dog's vocabulary, which facilitates communication and improves the owner's control. Also, specific tricks help prevent and resolve specific behavior problems. For example, by teaching the dog to fetch her toys, the dog learns carrying a toy makes the owner happy and, therefore, will be more likely to chew her toy than other inappropriate items.

More important, teaching tricks prompts owners to lighten up and train with a sunny disposition. Really, tricks should be no different from any other behaviors we put on cue. But they are. When teaching tricks, owners have a much sweeter attitude, which in turn motivates the dog and improves her willingness to comply. The dog feels tricks are a blast, but formal commands are a drag. In fact, tricks are so enjoyable, they may be used as rewards in training by asking the dog to come, sit and down-stay and then rollover for a tummy rub. Go on, try it: Crack a smile and even giggle when the dog promptly and willingly lies down and stays.

Most important, performing tricks prompts onlookers to smile and giggle. Many people are scared of dogs, especially large ones. And nothing can be more off-putting for a dog than to be constantly confronted by strangers who don't like her because of her size or the way she looks. Uneasy people put the dog on edge, causing her to back off and bark, only frightening people all the more. And so a vicious circle develops, with the people's fear fueling the dog's fear *and vice versa*. Instead, tie a pink ribbon to your dog's collar and practice all sorts of tricks on walks and in the park, and you will be pleasantly amazed how it changes people's attitudes toward your friendly dog. The dog's repertoire of tricks is limited only by the trainer's imagination. Below I have described three of my favorites:

SPEAK AND SHUSH

The training sequence involved in teaching a dog to bark on request is no different from that used when training any behavior on cue: request—lure—response—reward. As always, the secret of success lies in finding an effective lure. If the dog always barks at the doorbell, for example, say "Rover, speak!", have an accomplice ring the doorbell, then reward the dog for barking. After a few woofs, ask Rover to "Shush!", waggle a food treat under her nose (to entice her to sniff and thus to shush), praise her when quiet and eventually offer the treat as a reward. Alternate "Speak" and "Shush," progressively increasing the length of shush-time between each barking bout.

PLAY BOW

With the dog standing, say "Bow!" and lower the food lure (palm upwards) to rest between the dog's forepaws. Praise as the dog lowers

her forequarters and sternum to the ground (as when teaching the down), but then lure the dog to stand and offer the treat. On successive trials, gradually increase the length of time the dog is required to remain in the play bow posture in order to gain a food reward. If the dog's rear end collapses into a down, say nothing and offer no reward; simply start over.

BE A BEAR

With the dog sitting backed into a corner to prevent her from toppling over backwards, say "Be a bear!" With bent paw and palm down, raise a lure upwards and backwards along the top of the dog's muzzle. Praise the dog when she sits up on her haunches and offer the treat as a reward. To prevent the dog from standing on her hind legs, keep the lure closer to the dog's muzzle. On each trial, progressively increase the length of time the dog is required to sit up to receive a food reward. Since lure-reward training is so easy, teach the dog to stand and walk on her hind legs as well!

Teaching "Be a Bear"

chapter 9

Getting
Active
with your Dog

by Bardi McLennan

Once you and your dog have graduated from basic obedience training and are beginning to work together as a team, you can take part in the growing world of dog activities. There are so many fun things to do with your dog! Just remember, people and dogs don't always learn at the same pace, so don't be upset if you (or your dog) need more than two basic training courses before your team becomes operational. Even smart dogs don't go straight to college from kindergarten!

Just as there are events geared to certain types of dogs, so there are ones that are more appealing to certain types of people. In some activities, you give the commands and your dog does the work (upland game hunting is one example), while in others, such as agility, you'll both get a workout. You may want to aim for prestigious titles to add to your dog's name, or you may want nothing more than the sheer enjoyment of being around other people and their dogs. Passive or active, participation has its own rewards.

Consider your dog's physical capabilities when looking into any of the canine activities. It's easy to see that a Basset Hound is not built for the racetrack, nor would a Chihuahua be the breed of choice for pulling a sled. A loyal dog will attempt almost anything you ask him to do, so it is up to you to know your

All dogs seem to love playing flyball.

dog's limitations. A dog must be physically sound in order to compete at any level in athletic activities, and being mentally sound is a definite plus. Advanced age, however, may not be a deterrent. Many dogs still hunt and herd at ten or twelve years of age. It's entirely possible for dogs to be "fit at 50." Take your dog for a checkup, explain to your vet the type of activity you have in mind and be guided by his or her findings.

You needn't be restricted to breed-specific sports if it's only fun you're after. Certain AKC activities are limited to designated breeds; however, as each new trial, test or sport has grown in popularity, so has the variety of breeds encouraged to participate at a fun level.

But don't shortchange your fun, or that of your dog, by thinking only of the basic function of her breed. Once a dog has learned how to learn, she can be taught to do just about anything as long as the size of the dog is right for the job and you both think it is fun and rewarding. In other words, you are a team.

To get involved in any of the activities detailed in this chapter, look for the names and addresses of the organizations that sponsor them in Chapter 13. You can also ask your breeder or a local dog trainer for contacts.

You can compete in obedience trials with a well trained dog.

Official American Kennel Club Activities

The following tests and trials are some of the events sanctioned by the AKC and sponsored by various dog clubs. Your dog's expertise will be rewarded with impressive titles. You can participate just for fun, or be competitive and go for those awards.

OBEDIENCE

Training classes begin with pups as young as three months of age in kindergarten puppy training, then advance to pre-novice (all exercises on lead) and go on to novice, which is where you'll start off-lead work. In obedience classes dogs learn to sit, stay, heel and come through a variety of exercises. Once you've got the basics down, you can enter obedience trials and work toward earning your dog's first degree, a C.D. (Companion Dog).

The next level is called "Open," in which jumps and retrieves perk up the dog's interest. Passing grades in competition at this level earn a C.D.X. (Companion Dog Excellent). Beyond that lies the goal of the most ambitious—Utility (U.D. and even U.D.X. or OTCh, an Obedience Champion).

AGILITY

All dogs can participate in the latest canine sport to have gained worldwide popularity for its fun and excitement, agility. It began in England as a canine version of horse show-jumping, but because dogs are more agile and able to perform on verbal commands, extra feats were added such as climbing, balancing and racing through tunnels or in and out of weave poles. Many of the obstacles (regulation or homemade) can be set up in your own backyard. If the agility bug bites, you could end up in international competition!

For starters, your dog should be obedience trained, even though, in the beginning, the lessons may all be taught on lead. Once the dog understands the commands (and you do, too), it's as easy as guiding the dog over a prescribed course, one obstacle at a time. In competition, the race is against the clock, so wear your running shoes! The dog starts with 200 points and the judge deducts for infractions and misadventures along the way.

All dogs seem to love agility and respond to it as if they were being turned loose in a playground paradise. Your dog's enthusiasm will be contagious; agility turns into great fun for dog and owner.

FIELD TRIALS AND HUNTING TESTS

There are field trials and hunting tests for the sporting breeds—retrievers, spaniels and pointing breeds, and for some hounds—Bassets, Beagles and Dachshunds. Field trials are competitive events that test a dog's ability to perform the functions for which she was bred. Hunting tests, which are open to retrievers,

---

TITLES AWARDED BY THE AKC

Conformation: Ch. (Champion)

Obedience: CD (Companion Dog); CDX (Companion Dog Excellent); UD (Utility Dog); UDX (Utility Dog Excellent); OTCh. (Obedience Trial Champion)

Field: JH (Junior Hunter); SH (Senior Hunter); MH (Master Hunter); AFCh. (Amateur Field Champion); FCh. (Field Champion)

Lure Coursing: JC (Junior Courser); SC (Senior Courser)

Herding: HT (Herding Tested); PT (Pre-Trial Tested); HS (Herding Started); HI (Herding Intermediate); HX (Herding Excellent); HCh. (Herding Champion)

Tracking: TD (Tracking Dog); TDX (Tracking Dog Excellent)

Agility: NAD (Novice Agility); OAD (Open Agility); ADX (Agility Excellent); MAX (Master Agility)

Earthdog Tests: JE (Junior Earthdog); SE (Senior Earthdog); ME (Master Earthdog)

Canine Good Citizen: CGC

Combination: DC (Dual Champion—Ch. and Fch.); TC (Triple Champion—Ch., Fch., and OTCh.)

spaniels and pointing breeds only, are noncompetitive
and are a means of judging the dog's ability as well as
that of the handler.

Hunting is a very large and complex part of canine
sports, and if you own one of the breeds that hunts, the
events are a great treat for your dog and you. He gets
to do what he was bred for, and you get to work with
him and watch him do it. You'll be proud of and
amazed at what your dog can do.

*Retrievers and
other sporting
breeds get to do
what they're
bred to in hunt-
ing tests.*

Fortunately, the AKC publishes a series of booklets on
these events, which outline the rules and regulations
and include a glossary of the sometimes complicated
terms. The AKC also publishes newsletters for field tri-
alers and hunting test enthusiasts. The United Kennel
Club (UKC) also has informative materials for the
hunter and his dog.

HERDING TESTS AND TRIALS

Herding, like hunting, dates
back to the first known uses man
made of dogs. The interest in
herding today is widespread,
and if you own a herding breed,
you can join in the activity.
Herding dogs are tested for
their natural skills to keep a
flock of ducks, sheep or cattle
together. If your dog shows
potential, you can start at the
testing level, where your dog can
earn a title for showing an inherent herding ability.
With training you can advance to the trial level, where
your dog should be capable of controlling even difficult livestock in diverse situations.

LURE COURSING

The AKC Tests and Trials for Lure Coursing are open
to traditional sighthounds—Greyhounds, Whippets,

Borzoi, Salukis, Afghan Hounds, Ibizan Hounds and Scottish Deerhounds—as well as to Basenjis and Rhodesian Ridgebacks. Hounds are judged on overall ability, follow, speed, agility and endurance. This is possibly the most exciting of the trials for spectators, because the speed and agility of the dogs is awesome to watch as they chase the lure (or "course") in heats of two or three dogs at a time.

TRACKING

Tracking is another activity in which almost any dog can compete because every dog that sniffs the ground when taken outdoors is, in fact, tracking. The hard part comes when the rules as to what, when and where the dog tracks are determined by a person, not the dog! Tracking tests cover a large area of fields, woods and roads. The tracks are laid hours before the dogs go to work on them, and include "tricks" like cross-tracks and sharp turns. If you're interested in search-and-rescue work, this is the place to start.

This tracking dog is hot on the trail.

EARTHDOG TESTS FOR SMALL TERRIERS AND DACHSHUNDS

These tests are open to Australian, Bedlington, Border, Cairn, Dandie Dinmont, Smooth and Wire Fox, Lakeland, Norfolk, Norwich, Scottish, Sealyham, Skye, Welsh and West Highland White Terriers as well as Dachshunds. The dogs need no prior training for this terrier sport. There is a qualifying test on the day of the event, so dog and handler learn the rules on the spot. These tests, or "digs," sometimes end with informal races in the late afternoon.

Here are some of the extracurricular obedience and racing activities that are not regulated by the AKC or UKC, but are generally run by clubs or a group of dog fanciers and are often open to all.

Canine Freestyle This activity is something new on the scene and is variously likened to dancing, dressage or ice skating. It is meant to show the athleticism of the dog, but also requires showmanship on the part of the dog's handler. If you and your dog like to ham it up for friends, you might want to look into freestyle.

Lure coursing lets sighthounds do what they do best—run!

Scent Hurdle Racing Scent hurdle racing is purely a fun activity sponsored by obedience clubs with members forming competing teams. The height of the hurdles is based on the size of the shortest dog on the team. On a signal, one team dog is released on each of two side-by-side courses and must clear every hurdle before picking up its own dumbbell from a platform and returning over the jumps to the handler. As each dog returns, the next on that team is sent. Of course, that is what the dogs are supposed to do. When the dogs improvise (going under or around the hurdles, stealing another dog's dumbbell, and so forth), it no doubt frustrates the handlers, but just adds to the fun for everyone else.

Flyball This type of racing is similar, but after negotiating the four hurdles, the dog comes to a flyball box, steps on a lever that releases a tennis ball into the air, catches the ball and returns over the hurdles to the starting point. This game also becomes extremely fun for spectators because the dogs sometimes cheat by catching a ball released by the dog in the next lane. Three titles can be earned—Flyball Dog (F.D.), Flyball Dog Excellent (F.D.X.) and Flyball Dog Champion (Fb.D.Ch.)—all awarded by the North American Flyball Association, Inc.

Dogsledding The name conjures up the Rocky Mountains or the frigid North, but you can find dogsled clubs in such unlikely spots as Maryland, North Carolina and Virginia! Dogsledding is primarily for the Nordic breeds such as the Alaskan Malamutes, Siberian Huskies and Samoyeds, but other breeds can try. There are some practical backyard applications to this sport, too. With parental supervision, almost any strong dog could pull a child's sled.

Coming over the A-frame on an agility course.

These are just some of the many recreational ways you can get to know and understand your multifaceted dog better and have fun doing it.

chapter 10

Your Dog
and your
Family

by Bardi McLennan

Adding a dog automatically increases your family by one, no matter whether you live alone in an apartment or are part of a mother, father and six kids household. The single-person family is fair game for numerous and varied canine misconceptions as to who is dog and who pays the bills, whereas a dog in a houseful of children will consider himself to be just one of the gang, littermates all. One dog and one child may give a dog reason to believe they are both kids or both dogs.

Either interpretation requires parental supervision and sometimes speedy intervention.

As soon as one paw goes through the door into your home, Rufus (or Rufina) has to make many adjustments to become a part of your family. Your job is to make him fit in as painlessly as possible. An older dog may have some frame of reference from past experience, but to a 10-week-old puppy, everything is brand new: people, furniture, stairs, when and where people eat, sleep or watch TV, his own place and everyone else's space, smells, sounds, outdoors—everything!

Puppies, and newly acquired dogs of any age, do not need what we think of as "freedom." If you leave a new dog or puppy loose in the house, you will almost certainly return to chaotic destruction and the dog will forever after equate your homecoming with a time of punishment to be dreaded. It is unfair to give your dog what amounts to "freedom to get into trouble." Instead, confine him to a crate for brief periods of your absence (up to three or four hours) and, for the long haul, a workday for example, confine him to one untrashable area with his own toys, a bowl of water and a radio left on (low) in another room.

Lots of pets get along with each other just fine.

For the first few days, when not confined, put Rufus on a long leash tied to your wrist or waist. This umbilical cord method enables the dog to learn all about you from your body language and voice, and to learn by his own actions which things in the house are NO! and which ones are rewarded by "Good dog." House-training will be easier with the pup always by your side. Speaking of which, accidents do happen. That goal of "completely housetrained" takes up to a year, or the length of time it takes the pup to mature.

The All-Adult Family

Most dogs in an adults-only household today are likely to be latchkey pets, with no one home all day but the dog. When you return after a tough day on the job, the dog can and should be your relaxation therapy. But going home can instead be a daily frustration.

Separation anxiety is a very common problem for the dog in a working household. It may begin with whines and barks of loneliness, but it will soon escalate into a frenzied destruction derby. That is why it is so important to set aside the time to teach a dog to relax when left alone in his confined area and to understand that he can trust you to return.

Let the dog get used to your work schedule in easy stages. Confine him to one room and go in and out of that room over and over again. Be casual about it. No physical, voice or eye contact. When the pup no longer even notices your comings and goings, leave the house for varying lengths of time, returning to stay home for a few minutes and gradually increasing the time away. This training can take days, but the dog is learning that you haven't left him forever and that he can trust you.

Any time you leave the dog, but especially during this training period, be casual about your departure. No anxiety-building fond farewells. Just "Bye" and go! Remember the "Good dog" when you return to find everything more or less as you left it.

If things are a mess (or even a disaster) when you return, greet the dog, take him outside to eliminate, and then put him in his crate while you clean up. Rant and rave in the shower! *Do not* punish the dog. You were not there when it happened, and the rule is: Only punish as you catch the dog in the act of wrongdoing. Obviously, it makes sense to get your latchkey puppy when you'll have a week or two to spend on these training essentials.

Family weekend activities should include Rufus whenever possible. Depending on the pup's age, now is the time for a long walk in the park, playtime in the backyard, a hike in the woods. Socializing is as important as health care, good food and physical exercise, so visiting Aunt Emma or Uncle Harry and the next-door

neighbor's dog or cat is essential to developing an o
going, friendly temperament in your pet.

If you are a single adult, socializing Rufus at hor.
away will prevent him from becoming overly protect.
of you (or just overly attached) and will also prevent
such behavioral problems as dominance or fear of
strangers.

Babies

Whether already here or on the way, babies figure
larger than life in the eyes of a dog. If the dog is there
first, let him in on all your baby preparations in the
house. When baby arrives, let Rufus sniff any item of
clothing that has been on the baby before Junior
comes home. Then let Mom greet the dog first before
introducing the new family member. Hold the baby
down for the dog to see and sniff, but make sure someone's holding the dog on
lead in case of any sudden
moves. Don't play keep-
away or tease the dog with
the baby, which only
invites undesirable jump-
ing up.

Dogs are perfect confidants.

The dog and the baby are
"family," and for starters
can be treated almost
as equals. Things rapidly
change, however, espe-
cially when baby takes to
creeping around on all
fours on the dog's turf or,
better yet, has yummy
pudding all over her face
and hands! That's when a lot of things in the dog's and
baby's lives become more separate than equal.

Toddlers make terrible dog owners, but if you can't
avoid the combination, use patient discipline (that is,
positive teaching rather than punishment), and use
time-outs before you run out of patience.

A dog and a baby (or toddler, or an assertive young child) should never be left alone together. Take the dog with you or confine him. With a baby or youngsters in the house, you'll have plenty of use for that wonderful canine safety device called a crate!

Young Children

Any dog in a house with kids will behave pretty much as the kids do, good or bad. But even good dogs and good children can get into trouble when play becomes rowdy and active.

Legs bobbing up and down, shrill voices screeching, a ball hurtling overhead, all add up to exuberant frustration for a dog who's just trying to be part of the gang. In a pack of puppies, any legs or toys being chased would be caught by a set of teeth, and all the pups involved would understand that is how the game is played. Kids do not understand this, nor do parents tolerate it. Bring Rufus indoors before you have reason to regret it. This is time-out, not a punishment.

Teach children how to play nicely with a puppy.

You can explain the situation to the children and tell them they must play quieter games until the puppy learns not to grab them with his mouth. Unfortunately, you can't explain it that easily to the dog. With adult supervision, they will learn how to play together.

Young children love to tease. Sticking their faces or wiggling their hands or fingers in the dog's face is teasing. To another person it might be just annoying, but it is threatening to a dog. There's another difference: We can make the child stop by an explanation, but the only way a dog can stop it is with a warning growl and then with teeth. Teasing is the major cause of children being bitten by their pets. Treat it seriously.

Older Children

The best age for a child to get a first dog is between the ages of 8 and 12. That's when kids are able to accept some real responsibility for their pet. Even so, take the child's vow of "I will never *ever* forget to feed (brush, walk, etc.) the dog" for what it's worth: a child's good intention at that moment. Most kids today have extra lessons, soccer practice, Little League, ballet, and so forth piled on top of school schedules. There will be many times when Mom will have to come to the dog's rescue. "I walked the dog for you so you can set the table for me" is one way to get around a missed appointment without laying on blame or guilt.

Kids in this age group make excellent obedience trainers because they are into the teaching/learning process themselves and they lack the self-consciousness of adults. Attending a dog show is something the whole family can enjoy, and watching Junior Showmanship may catch the eye of the kids. Older children can begin to get involved in many of the recreational activities that were reviewed in the previous chapter. Some of the agility obstacles, for example, can be set up in the backyard as a family project (with an adult making sure all the equipment is safe and secure for the dog).

Older kids are also beginning to look to the future, and may envision themselves as veterinarians or trainers or show dog handlers or writers of the next Lassie best-seller. Dogs are perfect confidants for these dreams. They won't tell a soul.

Other Pets

Introduce all pets tactfully. In a dog/cat situation, hold the dog, not the cat. Let two dogs meet on neutral turf—a stroll in the park or a walk down the street—with both on loose leads to permit all the normal canine ways of saying hello, including routine sniffing, circling, more sniffing, and so on. Small creatures such as hamsters, chinchillas or mice must be kept safe from their natural predators (dogs and cats).

Festive Family Occasions

Parties are great for people, but not necessarily for puppies. Until all the guests have arrived, put the dog in his crate or in a room where he won't be disturbed. A socialized dog can join the fun later as long as he's not underfoot, annoying guests or into the hors d'oeuvres.

There are a few dangers to consider, too. Doors opening and closing can allow a puppy to slip out unnoticed in the confusion, and you'll be organizing a search party instead of playing host or hostess. Party food and buffet service are not for dogs. Let Rufus party in his crate with a nice big dog biscuit.

At Christmas time, not only are tree decorations dangerous and breakable (and perhaps family heirlooms), but extreme caution should be taken with the lights, cords and outlets for the tree lights and any other festive lighting. Occasionally a dog lifts a leg, ignoring the fact that the tree is indoors. To avoid this, use a canine repellent, made for gardens, on the tree. Or keep him out of the tree room unless supervised. And whatever you do, *don't* invite trouble by hanging his toys on the tree!

Car Travel

Before you plan a vacation by car or RV with Rufus, be sure he enjoys car travel. Nothing spoils a holiday quicker than a carsick dog! Work within the dog's comfort level. Get in the car with the dog in his crate or attached to a canine car safety belt and just sit there until he relaxes. That's all. Next time, get in the car, turn on the engine and go nowhere. Just sit. When that is okay, turn on the engine and go around the block. Now you can go for a ride and include a stop where you get out, leaving the dog for a minute or two.

On a warm day, always park in the shade and leave windows open several inches. And return quickly. It only takes 10 minutes for a car to become an overheated steel death trap.

Motel or Pet Motel?

Not all motels or hotels accept pets, but you have a much better choice today than even a few years ago. To find a dog-friendly lodging, look at *On the Road Again With Man's Best Friend*, a series of directories that detail bed and breakfasts, inns, family resorts and other hotels/motels. Some places require a refundable deposit to cover any damage incurred by the dog. More B&Bs accept pets now, but some restrict the size.

If taking Rufus with you is not feasible, check out boarding kennels in your area. Your veterinarian may offer this service, or recommend a kennel or two he or she is familiar with. Go see the facilities for yourself, ask about exercise, diet, housing, and so on. Or, if you'd rather have Rufus stay home, look into bonded petsitters, many of whom will also bring in the mail and water your plants.

chapter 11

Your Dog
and your
Community

by Bardi McLennan

Step outside your home with your dog and you are no longer just family, you are both part of your community. This is when the phrase "responsible pet ownership" takes on serious implications. For starters, it means you pick up after your dog—not just occasionally, but every time your dog eliminates away from home. That means you have joined the Plastic Baggy Brigade! You always have plastic sandwich bags in your pocket and several in the car. It means you teach your kids how to use them, too. If you think this is "yucky," just imagine what

the person (a non-doggy person) who inadvertently steps in the mess thinks!

Your responsibility extends to your neighbors: To their ears (no annoying barking); to their property (their garbage, their lawn, their flower beds, their cat—especially their cat); to their kids (on bikes, at play); to their kids' toys and sports equipment.

There are numerous dog-related laws, ranging from simple dog licensing and leash laws to those holding you liable for any physical injury or property damage done by your dog. These laws are in place to protect everyone in the community, including you and your dog. There are town ordinances and state laws which are by no means the same in all towns or all states. Ignorance of the law won't get you off the hook. The time to find out what the laws are where you live is now.

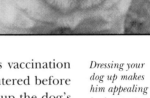

Be sure your dog's license is current. This is not just a good local ordinance, it can make the difference between finding your lost dog or not. Many states now require proof of rabies vaccination and that the dog has been spayed or neutered before issuing a license. At the same time, keep up the dog's annual immunizations.

Dressing your dog up makes him appealing to strangers.

Never let your dog run loose in the neighborhood. This will not only keep you on the right side of the leash law, it's the outdoor version of the rule about not giving your dog "freedom to get into trouble."

Good Canine Citizen

Sometimes it's hard for a dog's owner to assess whether or not the dog is sufficiently socialized to be accepted by the community at large. Does Rufus or Rufina display good, controlled behavior in public? The AKC's Canine Good Citizen program is available through many dog organizations. If your dog passes the test, the title "CGC" is earned.

The overall purpose is to turn your dog into a good neighbor and to teach you about your responsibility to your community as a dog owner. Here are the ten things your dog must do willingly:

1. Accept a stranger stopping to chat with you.
2. Sit and be petted by a stranger.
3. Allow a stranger to handle him or her as a groomer or veterinarian would.
4. Walk nicely on a loose lead.
5. Walk calmly through a crowd.
6. Sit and down on command, then stay in a sit or down position while you walk away.
7. Come when called.
8. Casually greet another dog.
9. React confidently to distractions.
10. Accept being left alone with someone other than you and not become overly agitated or nervous.

Schools and Dogs

Schools are getting involved with pet ownership on an educational level. It has been proven that children who are kind to animals are humane in their attitude toward other people as adults.

A dog is a child's best friend, and so children are often primary pet owners, if not the primary caregivers. Unfortunately, they are also the ones most often bitten by dogs. This occurs due to a lack of understanding that pets, no matter how sweet, cuddly and loving, are still animals. Schools, along with parents, dog clubs, dog fanciers and the AKC, are working to change all that with video programs for children not only in grade school, but in the nursery school and pre-kindergarten age group. Teaching youngsters how to be responsible dog owners is important community work. When your dog has a CGC, volunteer to take part in an educational classroom event put on by your dog club.

Boy Scout Merit Badge

A Merit Badge for Dog Care can be earned by any Boy Scout ages 11 to 18. The requirements are not easy, but amount to a complete course in responsible dog care and general ownership. Here are just a few of the things a Scout must do to earn that badge:

Point out ten parts of the dog using the correct names.

Give a report (signed by parent or guardian) on your care of the dog (feeding, food used, housing, exercising, grooming and bathing), plus what has been done to keep the dog healthy.

Explain the right way to obedience train a dog, and demonstrate three comments.

Several of the requirements have to do with health care, including first aid, handling a hurt dog, and the dangers of home treatment for a serious ailment.

The final requirement is to know the local laws and ordinances involving dogs.

There are similar programs for Girl Scouts and 4-H members.

Local Clubs

Local dog clubs are no longer in existence just to put on a yearly dog show. Today, they are apt to be the hub of the community's involvement with pets. Dog clubs conduct educational forums with big-name speakers, stage demonstrations of canine talent in a busy mall and take dogs of various breeds to schools for class-room discussion.

The quickest way to feel accepted as a member in a club is to volunteer your services! Offer to help with something—anything—and watch your popularity (and your interest) grow.

Therapy Dogs

Once your dog has earned that essential CGC and reliably demonstrates a steady, calm temperament, you could look into what therapy dogs are doing in your area.

Therapy dogs go with their owners to visit patients at hospitals or nursing homes, generally remaining on leash but able to coax a pat from a stiffened hand, a smile from a blank face, a few words from sealed lips or a hug from someone in need of love.

Nursing homes cover a wide range of patient care. Some specialize in care of the elderly, some in the treatment of specific illnesses, some in physical therapy. Children's facilities also welcome visits from trained therapy dogs for boosting morale in their pediatric patients. Hospice care for the terminally ill and the at-home care of AIDS patients are other areas where this canine visiting is desperately needed. Therapy dog training comes first.

Your dog can make a difference in lots of lives.

There is a lot more involved than just taking your nice friendly pooch to someone's bedside. Doing therapy dog work involves your own emotional stability as well as that of your dog. But once you have met all the requirements for this work, making the rounds once a week or once a month with your therapy dog is possibly the most rewarding of all community activities.

Disaster Aid

This community service is definitely not for everyone, partly because it is time-consuming. The initial training is rigorous, and there can be no let-up in the continuing workouts, because members are on call 24 hours a day to go wherever they are needed at a moment's notice. But if you think you would like to be able to assist in a disaster, look into search-and-rescue work. The network of search-and-rescue volunteers is worldwide, and all members of the American Rescue Dog Association (ARDA) who are qualified to do this work are volunteers who train and maintain their own dogs.

Physical Aid

Most people are familiar with Seeing Eye dogs, which serve as blind people's eyes, but not with all the other work that dogs are trained to do to assist the disabled. Dogs are also specially trained to pull wheelchairs, carry school books, pick up dropped objects, open and close doors. Some also are ears for the deaf. All these assistance-trained dogs, by the way, are allowed anywhere "No Pet" signs exist (as are therapy dogs when properly identified). Getting started in any of this fascinating work requires a background in dog training and canine behavior, but there are also volunteer jobs ranging from answering the phone to cleaning out kennels to providing a foster home for a puppy. You have only to ask.

Making the rounds with your therapy dog can be very rewarding.

part four

Beyond the Basics

chapter 12

Recommended Reading

Books

ABOUT HEALTH CARE

Ackerman, Lowell. *Guide to Skin and Haircoat Problems in Dogs.* Loveland, Colo.: Alpine Publications, 1994.

Alderton, David. *The Dog Care Manual.* Hauppauge, N.Y.: Barron's Educational Series, Inc., 1986.

American Kennel Club. *American Kennel Club Dog Care and Training.* New York: Howell Book House, 1991.

Bamberger, Michelle, DVM. *Help! The Quick Guide to First Aid for Your Dog.* New York: Howell Book House, 1995.

Carlson, Delbert, DVM, and James Giffin, MD. *Dog Owner's Home Veterinary Handbook.* New York: Howell Book House, 1992.

DeBitetto, James, DVM, and Sarah Hodgson. *You & Your Puppy.* New York: Howell Book House, 1995.

Humphries, Jim, DVM. *Dr. Jim's Animal Clinic for Dogs.* New York: Howell Book House, 1994.

McGinnis, Terri. *The Well Dog Book.* New York: Random House, 1991.

Pitcairn, Richard and Susan. *Natural Health for Dogs.* Emmaus, Pa.: Rodale Press, 1982.

ABOUT DOG SHOWS

Hall, Lynn. *Dog Showing for Beginners.* New York: Howell Book House, 1994.

Nichols, Virginia Tuck. *How to Show Your Own Dog.* Neptune, N. J.: TFH, 1970.

Vanacore, Connie. *Dog Showing, An Owner's Guide.* New York: Howell Book House, 1990.

About Training

Ammen, Amy. *Training in No Time.* New York: Howell Book House, 1995.

Baer, Ted. *Communicating With Your Dog.* Hauppauge, N.Y.: Barron's Educational Series, Inc., 1989.

Benjamin, Carol Lea. *Dog Problems.* New York: Howell Book House, 1989.

Benjamin, Carol Lea. *Dog Training for Kids.* New York: Howell Book House, 1988.

Benjamin, Carol Lea. *Mother Knows Best.* New York: Howell Book House, 1985.

Benjamin, Carol Lea. *Surviving Your Dog's Adolescence.* New York: Howell Book House, 1993.

Bohnenkamp, Gwen. *Manners for the Modern Dog.* San Francisco: Perfect Paws, 1990.

Dibra, Bashkim. *Dog Training by Bash.* New York: Dell, 1992.

Dunbar, Ian, PhD, MRCVS. *Dr. Dunbar's Good Little Dog Book,* James & Kenneth Publishers, 2140 Shattuck Ave. #2406, Berkeley, Calif. 94704. (510) 658–8588. Order from the publisher.

Dunbar, Ian, PhD, MRCVS. *How to Teach a New Dog Old Tricks,* James & Kenneth Publishers. Order from the publisher; address above.

Dunbar, Ian, PhD, MRCVS, and Gwen Bohnenkamp. Booklets on *Preventing Aggression; Housetraining; Chewing; Digging; Barking; Socialization; Fearfulness; and Fighting,* James & Kenneth Publishers. Order from the publisher; address above.

Evans, Job Michael. *People, Pooches and Problems.* New York: Howell Book House, 1991.

Kilcommons, Brian and Sarah Wilson. *Good Owners, Great Dogs.* New York: Warner Books, 1992.

McMains, Joel M. *Dog Logic—Companion Obedience.* New York: Howell Book House, 1992.

Rutherford, Clarice and David H. Neil, MRCVS. *How to Raise a Puppy You Can Live With.* Loveland, Colo.: Alpine Publications, 1982.

Volhard, Jack and Melissa Bartlett. *What All Good Dogs Should Know: The Sensible Way to Train.* New York: Howell Book House, 1991.

About Breeding

Harris, Beth J. Finder. *Breeding a Litter, The Complete Book of Prenatal and Postnatal Care.* New York: Howell Book House, 1983.

Holst, Phyllis, DVM. *Canine Reproduction.* Loveland, Colo.: Alpine Publications, 1985.

Walkowicz, Chris and Bonnie Wilcox, DVM. *Successful Dog Breeding, The Complete Handbook of Canine Midwifery*. New York: Howell Book House, 1994.

ABOUT ACTIVITIES

American Rescue Dog Association. *Search and Rescue Dogs*. New York: Howell Book House, 1991.

Barwig, Susan and Stewart Hilliard. *Schutzhund*. New York: Howell Book House, 1991.

Beaman, Arthur S. *Lure Coursing*. New York: Howell Book House, 1994.

Daniels, Julie. *Enjoying Dog Agility—From Backyard to Competition*. New York: Doral Publishing, 1990.

Davis, Kathy Diamond. *Therapy Dogs*. New York: Howell Book House, 1992.

Gallup, Davis Anne. *Running With Man's Best Friend*. Loveland, Colo.: Alpine Publications, 1986.

Habgood, Dawn and Robert. *On the Road Again With Man's Best Friend*. New England, Mid-Atlantic, West Coast and Southeast editions. Selective guides to area bed and breakfasts, inns, hotels and resorts that welcome guests and their dogs. New York: Howell Book House, 1995.

Holland, Vergil S. *Herding Dogs*. New York: Howell Book House, 1994.

LaBelle, Charlene G. *Backpacking With Your Dog*. Loveland, Colo.: Alpine Publications, 1993.

Simmons-Moake, Jane. *Agility Training, The Fun Sport for All Dogs*. New York: Howell Book House, 1991.

Spencer, James B. *Hup! Training Flushing Spaniels the American Way*. New York: Howell Book House, 1992.

Spencer, James B. *Point! Training the All-Seasons Birddog*. New York: Howell Book House, 1995.

Tarrant, Bill. *Training the Hunting Retriever*. New York: Howell Book House, 1991.

Volhard, Jack and Wendy. *The Canine Good Citizen*. New York: Howell Book House, 1994.

General Titles

Haggerty, Captain Arthur J. *How to Get Your Pet Into Show Business*. New York: Howell Book House, 1994.

McLennan, Bardi. *Dogs and Kids, Parenting Tips*. New York: Howell Book House, 1993.

Moran, Patti J. *Pet Sitting for Profit, A Complete Manual for Professional Success*. New York: Howell Book House, 1992.

Scalisi, Danny and Libby Moses. *When Rover Just Won't Do, Over 2,000 Suggestions for Naming Your Dog.* New York: Howell Book House, 1993.

Sife, Wallace, PhD. *The Loss of a Pet.* New York: Howell Book House, 1993.

Wrede, Barbara J. *Civilizing Your Puppy.* Hauppauge, N.Y.: Barron's Educational Series, 1992.

Magazines

The AKC GAZETTE, The Official Journal for the Sport of Purebred Dogs. American Kennel Club, 51 Madison Ave., New York, NY.

Bloodlines Journal. United Kennel Club, 100 E. Kilgore Rd., Kalamazoo, MI.

Dog Fancy. Fancy Publications, 3 Burroughs, Irvine, CA 92718

Dog World. Maclean Hunter Publishing Corp., 29 N. Wacker Dr., Chicago, IL 60606.

Videos

"SIRIUS Puppy Training," by Ian Dunbar, PhD, MRCVS. James & Kenneth Publishers, 2140 Shattuck Ave. #2406, Berkeley, CA 94704. Order from the publisher.

"Training the Companion Dog," from Dr. Dunbar's British TV Series, James & Kenneth Publishers. (See address above).

The American Kennel Club produces videos on every breed of dog, as well as on hunting tests, field trials and other areas of interest to purebred dog owners. For more information, write to AKC/Video Fulfillment, 5580 Centerview Dr., Suite 200, Raleigh, NC 27606.

chapter 13

Resources

Breed Clubs

Every breed recognized by the American Kennel Club has a national (parent) club. National clubs are a great source of information on your breed. You can get the name of the secretary of the club by contacting:

The American Kennel Club
51 Madison Avenue
New York, NY 10010
(212) 696-8200

There are also numerous all-breed, individual breed, obedience, hunting and other special-interest dog clubs across the country. The American Kennel Club can provide you with a geographical list of clubs to find ones in your area. Contact them at the above address.

Registry Organizations

Registry organizations register purebred dogs. The American Kennel Club is the oldest and largest in this country, and currently recognizes over 130 breeds. The United Kennel Club registers some breeds the AKC doesn't (including the American Pit Bull Terrier and the Miniature Fox Terrier) as well as many of the same breeds. The others included here are for your reference; the AKC can provide you with a list of foreign registries.

American Kennel Club
51 Madison Avenue
New York, NY 10010

United Kennel Club (UKC)
100 E. Kilgore Road
Kalamazoo, MI 49001-5598

American Dog Breeders Assn.
P.O. Box 1771
Salt Lake City, UT 84110
(Registers American Pit Bull Terriers)

Canadian Kennel Club
89 Skyway Avenue
Etobicoke, Ontario
Canada M9W 6R4

National Stock Dog Registry
P.O. Box 402
Butler, IN 46721
(Registers working stock dogs)

Orthopedic Foundation for Animals (OFA)
2300 E. Nifong Blvd.
Columbia, MO 65201-3856
(Hip registry)

Activity Clubs

Write to these organizations for information on the
activities they sponsor.

American Kennel Club
51 Madison Avenue
New York, NY 10010
(Conformation Shows, Obedience Trials, Field
Trials and Hunting Tests, Agility, Canine Good

Citizen, Lure Coursing, Herding, Tracking, Earthdog Tests, Coonhunting.)

United Kennel Club
100 E. Kilgore Road
Kalamazoo, MI 49001-5598
(Conformation Shows, Obedience Trials, Agility,
Hunting for Various Breeds, Terrier Trials and
more.)

North American Flyball Assn.
1342 Jeff St.
Ypsilanti, MI 48198

International Sled Dog Racing Assn.
P.O. Box 446
Norman, ID 83848-0446

North American Working Dog Assn., Inc.
Southeast Kreisgruppe
P.O. Box 833
Brunswick, GA 31521

Trainers

Association of Pet Dog Trainers
P.O. Box 3734
Salinas, CA 93912
(408) 663–9257

American Dog Trainers' Network
161 West 4th St.
New York, NY 10014
(212) 727–7257

**National Association of Dog Obedience
Instructors**
2286 East Steel Rd.
St. Johns, MI 48879

Associations

American Dog Owners Assn.
1654 Columbia Tpk.
Castleton, NY 12033
(Combats anti-dog legislation)

Delta Society
P.O. Box 1080
Renton, WA 98057-1080
(Promotes the human/animal bond through
pet-assisted therapy and other programs)

Dog Writers Assn. of America (DWAA)
Sally Cooper, Secy.
222 Woodchuck Ln.
Harwinton, CT 06791

National Assn. for Search and Rescue (NASAR)
P.O. Box 3709
Fairfax, VA 22038

Therapy Dogs International
6 Hilltop Road
Mendham, NJ 07945